A NEW REALITY:

A WAKE UP CALL TO LIFE'S MYSTERIES.
by A.J. Aaron

A New Reality

The story that follows is true. In an effort to safeguard the privacy of individuals whose lives are reflected herein, all of the names and many identifying details of the people mentioned in this book have been changed. The publisher and author do not have any control over and does not assume responsibility for third party websites or their content.

A.J. Aaron

Contents

Introduction

Dr. M. Scott Peck wrote in his book, <u>The Road Less Traveled and Beyond</u>, pg 44, 1997 New York, Simon and Schuster: "How often, in fact, do we stop to think about what we believe? One of the major dilemmas we face both as individuals and as a society is simplistic thinking-or the failure to think at all. It isn't just a problem, it is the problem."

If you think about it, there are many instances where people just don't think. Look around at work, while driving, at the store. Once you see it in others, you may notice yourself not thinking as well. I know I have. How many times do people go to the doctor and receive treatment for their symptoms but never ask about what the root cause is that can be eliminated. Maybe a change in diet can eliminate the acid reflux. Or how many times have you seen someone picking the worst of four available exits out of a gas station to try to make a left turn from, like the one closest to the corner where they can't pull in behind traffic?

Dr. Peck also wrote:

"Of course people are different, but many make up their minds-even about important issues-on the basis of very little information except what society tells them is "normal". Given a choice, most opt not to think things through. They take the easy way out, buying into simplistic assumptions and stereotypes" (pg 33).

1

A New Reality

When strange things started happening to me, I had plenty to think about. Most people with whom I tried to discuss my thoughts resisted because what I expressed to them was completely different from what they knew as "normal." They pushed me away and encouraged me to ignore these new experiences and the information I found that may help explain them. But I had to think about what was happening to me, for my own sanity, even though everything I felt was not "normal" according to my own beliefs and values. I had very difficult questions that needed answers:

- Why did I meet a total stranger after dreaming of her and sharing a series of coincidences with her? How was I immediately intimate with this stranger, not physically, but on a higher level than I've ever experienced before?

- Did this person experience, what many would consider, a miracle directly related to our meeting and friendship? Or was this miracle a result of her being in the right place at the right time, or random chance, or maybe even through some strange divine power?

- How could we share the same thoughts and feelings at any given moment, answering each other's thoughts in physical reality?

- How can I see, hear, feel and sense things unheard of in my "normal" world?

I realized my previous paradigms did not apply anymore and I had to find a logical explanation for what was happening to me. These new experiences contradicted what I was raised to believe and what society, as a whole, accepted. This was impossible! Was I taught incorrectly and society's beliefs were based on invalid assumptions? I was completely confused.

I began to research these occurrences and found a wealth of information, some of which I share in this book. By using the knowledge I obtained from different sources and some of the greatest thinkers of our age, I attempt to explain my experiences in this book so you, the reader, can understand what was happening. The amazing part of obtaining this information was that it always seemed to show itself **after** whatever experience or question I had that needed an answer to occurred, not before. This was even stranger at times than the occurrence!

I changed the names of the people involved in this story, even my own, due to the nature of the beliefs held by society, but the events are entirely true. Even though some conversations or situations have been altered in the spirit of entertainment, this book is a depiction of actual events that occurred in my life. In order to put these happenings in perspective, you need to know who I am.

I am not a philosopher nor do I have an overly active imagination. Drugs or alcohol did not cook my brain. At the time these events started occurring, I was in fact, a conservative Catholic who graduated with honors from a prestigious east coast engineering school and the plant manager of a Fortune 500 manufacturing company. I was not driven by emotions or intuition, but by logic, numbers and deductions.

A New Reality

I was born in 1957 and raised by sons and daughters of Polish immigrants in a New England industrial town. Most people who lived in this town added "Ski" after the town's name due to the heavy amount of Polish immigrants that lived there. Grandparents on both sides of my family had Polish lineage to Polish peasant farmers. They instilled a strong Catholic faith into their children who in turn, raised me the same. My conservative, Catholic upbringing was full of guilt and fear of consequences if the strict rules were broken. No meat on Fridays and if you missed church on Sunday, you committed a sin equivalent to murder! These and similar values served me well and I stayed out of trouble because I feared God and anything that was not "normal," which was defined so meticulously throughout my childhood.

My parents were hard working, loving and logical, wanting nothing more than to see their sons succeed. Both my brother and I worked hard in school to make our parents proud and became the first descendants of our peasant grandparents to receive Bachelor of Science Degrees in Mechanical Engineering. Mechanical Engineering is an area based on the physical sciences and is deeply rooted in logic where only things that can be proven are real.

Naturally, with this type of education, one is skeptical of anything spiritual or mystical. My roommates in college and other engineers I knew even decided there wasn't a God or at least weren't sure of His existence. This certainly is not the type of background that would spark a person's curiosity in an intangible reality but rather a disbelief in anything similar. Needless to say, events that started to happen like meeting the stranger or feeling energy throughout my body for example, made me feel utterly out of synch. This was unexplainable by engineering or logical thinking. Was I insane? I felt as though I lost touch with reality and my imagination was taking over. I was extremely close to leaping from my logical, sane world into the world of insanity.

Magically though, I started to find answers to my questions from not only people who appeared in my life, but in books I felt compelled to buy but didn't open until months or years later. When I felt the need to open one of these books, the answer stared up at me from the print, even if I opened to a random page. This craziness started to make sense, or at least become believable to a man who would have considered these events to be anything but genuine.

Synchronistic events occur to bring you and another person together for a moment or a phrase. Coincidences that seem to occur at just the right time as the need presents itself. There is just enough normalcy in these to make you feel maybe you aren't entirely insane and yet maybe there really are more ways to live other than entirely by logic and reasoning since the occurrence seems so at odds with chance. Kinda makes you say, "Holy shit! Did that just happen?"

In this book, I do my best to convey important and useful information, although in the past, I found no pleasure in writing or reading. Writing never helped me feel better and it certainly was not enjoyable to this engineering mind. But lately, writing has helped me compose my thoughts and feelings while reading has helped me understand what has been occurring in my life thus far. Now, for some reason, I enjoy both and feel compelled to share my thoughts and feelings with others who may be struggling with their sanity as I have. This change in myself, strongly suggests I was meant to share my story in the hopes someone else, like me, finds this book at the right time in their life and are reassured they are not insane, but merely confused because of the limitations set by societal or their own paradigms.

Now I begin my story. If you have had strange phenomenon happen in your life or if you are just a "thinking" person, I hope you are comforted, or gain insight, as the case may be for you, as you read each page. When you finish, I hope you agree that there's more to life then what we see on the surface of our daily lives. Once the blinders we have put on ourselves, through our beliefs, and the beliefs of others, are removed, we can see the true reality of what we are and where we live. Enjoy my story.

I-Chin!?

"Common sense is the collection of prejudices
acquired by age eighteen."
-Albert Einstein

"You have some sort of mechanical bridge. I'm not sure how you're doing it but you are pulling it from somewhere," Brad said as he pushed his thick glasses back and sipped his beer and cola. He continued to speak rapidly, nodding animatedly.

"I don't know how you ever got into your career in manufacturing. You're such a high degree empathy, yet work in an environment that is pure logic. Nonetheless, you're very good at it."

He ran his hand over his sparse hair, sweeping back the lonely locks. His academic, professor-like looks earned him the nickname "Frasier," after the television star, which he closely resembled. The pedantic nomenclature he used was a combination of his Bachelors Degree in Psychology, his travels as a military brat and his studies in Chemistry and Biology. He had an IQ of 185, which is well above the 135 IQ minimum for admission to The Mensa's, a club for geniuses.

"Pulling what Brad? What am I pulling?" I begged Brad to enlighten me.

A New Reality

"Energy. Energy is the stuff that allows you to cover so many things in one day. You aren't just getting it from caffeine you know."

Since I respected Brad's knowledge I accepted what he said. Brad looked out the door of the bar and thought to himself for a moment. All of his animation ceased. He seemed to be frozen while he stared, like a computer downloading data. All of a sudden he came back to life and turned in his bar stool so we were facing each other. He pulled his bar stool back and straightened his posture, closing his eyes like an old-fashioned doll laying down for a nap. He rubbed his palms together and rotated them toward the floor and up again, cupping them at the same time. As he continued this ritual, I saw his enormous, light, blue eyes open wide behind those thick lenses. He looked straight into my eyes. I was confused at what he just did but once again accepted him as my teacher,

"Okay, now put your hand out, palms up and cupped. Good. Now bring them together as if you're holding a basketball-sized object made of water. Good!"

He then gave me this "thing" from between his hands. It felt resilient against my compressing touch. It was a tangible, touchable object that I couldn't see. It was like holding a balloon in my hands, yet it didn't have the feel of rubber around it. I completely felt it compress when I squeezed it between my hands but there was nothing to see! This "thing" was an object without objective reality to it, tangible, but not visible. I opened my hands and felt it slip away. With a total look of confusion on my face, I looked at Brad and asked, "What was that!?"

Brad explained, "That was what your mechanical bridge is bringing you. It's simple energy. There are other ways to get it too. It's something called 'Chi.' I'll bring you something to read about it."

The next day, Brad handed me some papers that were obviously photo copied many times. The copies seemed to have been passed on multiple times, only being copied from the original text once. The text described an exercise called "I-Chin" and described this particular version as being the most ancient form of this exercise known. There were many other versions of this form in varying degrees but this one was the one many others were based on.

I read the information Brad passed on to me at home that night. According to the instructions, the first step was to take cotton in your hands and remember how it felt. The instructions also pointed out there was no point attempting the exercises unless you can imagine what cotton feels like without physically touching it. As much as I thought this was nuts, for some reason I trusted Brad. So I practiced feeling the feel of cotton in my hand, alternating between the real thing and my mind on and off for weeks until finally, I did it perfectly.

One night, I decided I was ready to try the exercises. Even though they were not physically exerting, I generated a substantial amount of heat in my body, which grew as each exercise was performed in the order presented in the instructions. I was in the

recroom with my seven-year-old daughter and five-year-old son.
They laughed at the way I looked as I concentrated on the exercises.
I was not laughing at all by the time I was through. I was shocked!
The whole series took about forty-five minutes but it was the last two
exercises that astounded me!

My wife, Sadie, looked at me curiously as I tried to explain
to her what happened.

"When I did the second to last exercise where I imagined
pulling both thumbs back as they pointed into the solar plexus
region..." I demonstrated as I spoke, moving my hands to the
position where I imagined pulling my thumbs back.

"...I felt a rush of electric energy pushing in and out of the
pit of my stomach, radiating from my thumbs. It wasn't unpleasant
like feeling an actual electric shock. No, it was more like the chill
you get when something really hits home in a movie or a chill from a
realization of some kind. Yet more than that, a vibration that runs
through you. It filled me and alerted my senses, but I wasn't afraid
nor did I feel warned against something."

"A rush of electricity?" Sadie asked.

"Yes, a tremendous rush of electricity, or something that felt
like it. It's so difficult to put this sensation into words, but it was
real, like an electric shock without the unpleasantness. It made me
pay attention, but it didn't incur fear or my flight response. I felt as if
it pushed me backwards as it entered my body. Then, I did the last
exercise."

I motioned with my hands, showing Sadie how I did it. I raised my hands from my side, palms up, and imagined my arms rising up.

"A cool rush flowed over my body. All the heat generated from the exercises dissipated. It felt like cold air flowing over me, no, through me."

"How do you feel now?" Sadie asked.

"Relaxed, comfortable, curious, confused I guess."

"Do you think it will help you quit smoking?"

"I don't know but it sure is interesting."

I slept well that night and woke up feeling refreshed. I seemed to have more energy than normal and I usually had plenty of it anyways. When I got to work, I found time to talk to Brad about what happened.

"Wanna have a cup of coffee?" I asked.

"Twist my arm, will ya! Okay."

The background sounds of the horizontal presses beating away at their hydraulic tubing along with the screw machines cutting barstock into pieces parts drowned out the slight grinding noise of the coffee machine. We had to bend down and watch the cup to see the progress. Brad watched his cup fill up and I followed our coffee machine ritual. I motioned towards the door and he followed me outside to a quieter spot where we could actually have a conversation and I could grab a smoke. The sounds of the plant faded as we approached the exit and became quiet when the door closed behind us.

Brad was smiling at me inquisitively, trying to figure out what I was up to. He didn't speak, but I wasn't going to let him speak anyways. I only had a few minutes to explain what I experienced and I wanted an answer now.

I started, "I did those I-Chin exercises last night."

"Did you do them all?"

"Yeah, it took about forty-five minutes."

"Did they relax you?"

"I guess, but something happened while I was doing them that you didn't tell me about and neither did the text. I got pretty heated up even though there was no real physical exercise and at the end, I got this tremendous surge of, uh, what felt like electricity into me with each pull of my thumbs. The last part of the series gave me a rush of coolness that washed over me."

"Oh no! Now I've given a bazooka to someone who can't even aim it!" Brad cried out, laughing.

He continued, "You shouldn't have gotten to that stage for a while, maybe a year or two or three! Some people never get to that stage! I need to get a master to teach you."

"You're my teacher."

"NO, you need a MASTER!"

"Give me a book. I don't want to take classes or go to a 'MASTER!' What do you mean a bazooka!?" I asked as I lit another smoke. "Can it hurt someone, or me?"

"No, don't worry. You can't hurt anyone with it, or hurt yourself. Not you, that is. It's not in your nature at least. I just meant

12

the bazooka as descriptive of the power you've tapped. You've connected to the Chi. Very good! You can quit smoking with it, you know." Brad said as he pointed to my cigarette.

"Hmmm, did you speak to my wife about this?" I replied, not really wanting to quit anyway. "We'll see."

"Nope, didn't talk to mom."

I checked my watch and realized I had another meeting to go to.

"Thanks Brad. I'll talk to you later."

"Thanks for the coffee. Later."

"Yup."

I didn't get to think about our conversation, even for a minute, with the flurry of problems and business going on, until a few days later when my wife and kids left to visit family in Maine. I just made a trip there in July and spent time with everyone in the family so I didn't go this time. Not wanting to use another week of vacation, I stayed home and went to work each day.

The level of activity was high, as usual and we had even broken a shipping record last month. To celebrate this achievement, we had luncheons on all three shifts in the parking lot. The party tent was huge and decorated in a Mexican theme including food and alcohol free Margaritas. As the Plant Manager, it was my responsibility to attend each luncheon on every shift. What fun, eh? Sure, fun if you didn't have to go to all the parties!

My schedule for the next couple days was grueling. I had to go home at 6:00 pm the night before the first party started to get some sleep. Then I had to go back to work at 2:30 am for a meeting and then mingle at the party until 4:00 am. I went home to grab a nap only to come back to work a couple of hours later and catch up on paperwork, go to a meeting at 10:30 am, then party at noon. I had time after the luncheon to check my voicemails, emails and have some discussions before going to another meeting at 6:00 pm followed by partying and mingling until 7:30 pm. I felt like I do whenever I change my sleep patterns...shitty!

I felt tired, foggy and shaky, but of course not sleepy when I needed to be. I returned home about 8:00 pm, knowing I had to get some sleep and get back into the synch of regular sleep patterns so I can wake up at 6:00 am to start a new day. I changed my clothes and washed up. I fixed myself a drink and put on some music. I was certainly not prepared for what was happened next.

A.J. Aaron

Meditation

One of my favorite albums (CD's) was playing. It had a mixture of power and softness to it. I must have played it hundreds of times by now.

I sat on the loveseat in the recroom looking out the east window to the backyard. I could feel my heartbeat begin to slow from my hurried efforts to set myself up to relax. The ice cubes in the gin and tonic clinked in the glass with my company's logo on it as I raised it for a deep sip. The tart and bitter flavor felt refreshing as it flowed over my parched tongue. The loveseat felt exceptionally comfortable to me now, its coarse fabric under my left hand. The familiar smell of home helped me to relax further.

I mentally went through the events of the day and did a cursory planning of tomorrow in my mind. The appointments, the follow ups from the three shifts of conversation with two hundred and fifty people and so on. I was about halfway into my drink when I completed the task and started to fall prey to the influence of the music.

The music intrigued and delighted me. I always used music to help me feel the way I wanted to feel at any given time. This music gave me a feeling I can't really describe. Somewhat light and carefree, yet powerful and strong. Almost a contradiction.

"Color is the meter to the soul," the song said and, "Music creates the body line."

15

A New Reality

"Hmm." I thought. As I sat there relaxing, I thought about the sensation from the I-Chin exercises.

"Make yourself feel like you're holding cotton." I thought.

I started to do that, thinking maybe I could draw that electric sensation without doing all the exercises. I thought about my muscles and making sure they were all relaxed. Yes, all my muscles were relaxed. I took some deep breaths and closed my eyes, trying to slow my breathing and feel the "cotton" feel. The music played on in the background of my mind. My breathing slowed and became very shallow and I could feel my heart rate slow. My muscles contracted and my pants loosened around them as they did. An itch on my face came and left as I ignored it. I tried to feel the electric feeling. My breath was slow and shallow, so slow it felt there was no air moving in and out my nose. My heart felt as if it beat lazily.

Suddenly there came a flow of that electric feeling, a pulse of sorts, flowing through my feet and hands and through my torso. It was incredible, vibrating. My eyes were still shut but I could see a play of colors before me: vivid purple, hot pink and blue, blue. The hot pink seemed to be most prevalent, and long lasting, as well as the most pleasurable to me.

It felt as if I slipped down, not physically, but mentally, as if you were sleeping and then felt one of those jerks where your whole body jolts. Almost like dreaming you're falling and waking with a jolt. I didn't wake though, but felt as if I had entered some other place after I shifted, or slipped, down. I started to get excited and tried to analyze what was going on, then I lost it all.

There I sat, eyes open, still and relaxed, reaching for the rest of my drink. The ice was gone now and it was no longer cold. The music was still playing but I had put it on repeat anyway so I wouldn't have to get up. I looked at the clock on the mantel. A whole hour had transpired.

I could have sworn I was in the colors and had the electric feeling for just a few minutes, yet a whole hour had passed! I hadn't fallen asleep and I didn't get that tiredness you experience from a short nap. I guessed I had felt the Chi and seen the colors the whole time. Was this what happened when you meditated? I must have meditated I guessed. I had to learn more about this! I had one more drink and went to bed.

The next day I went into work and thought about the feeling I felt last night and what happened. When I hit the plant floor I could feel it again. It was coming up through the floor, through my feet, through my hands, and into me. It seemed to change intensity as I passed through different areas of the plant. Wow! I could feel the Chi as I walked. I wasn't even meditating or doing I-Chin but somehow I still connected to it.

At some point it went away. Probably during conversations as I got involved in the day. I noticed though if I relaxed I could call it back again. Interesting, but what could I do with it? Was I just over tired from yesterday and letting my imagination get the best of me? I started to worry about myself. As the fear moved in I felt the sensation subside and once again felt the thickness of my limbs and the weight of my body as I moved about.

"Brad, I need to speak with you."

"Yes you do A.J."

"How 'bout a beer tonight?"

"Sure, meet you there."

The day flew by as usual with its mixture of personnel, people, delivery and production problems: the politics of business going on about its stumbling way of trying to survive in the chosen industry we were in, the self centered goals of the individuals trying to mesh with each other to achieve the overall goals of the company. When the final fire was put out and it was past the time of required presence, I passed the business paper I subscribed to on to an engineer who cared for it more than I, closed my briefcase and shut down my computer.

I went out into the sunshine and warmth of the day, and found my car and drove off to the local watering hole to meet Brad. As I pulled past the front window I could see him in a seat at our corner of the bar. I parked in back and walked into the cool, somewhat dark, environment of our traditional meeting place of eighteen years. This was a place for celebrations, consultations, mediations and consolations for many a fellow employee, a place to be alone or to be together.

"Hi Tommy, how ya doin'!?' I shouted to the bartender as I walked to my seat.

"Good A.J! Still busy at work?" He replied as he pulled my brand from the cooler, and clinked it a few times as he worked to open it on the jig on the cooler.

"Yeah, too busy. Total chaos for all seven days a week."

"Hey guy." Brad said as I sat.

"Draft and a cola for Brad please Tommy."

"K man. How ya doin Brad?" Tommy said sarcastically.

"K Tommy."

I leaned over to him and spoke quietly.

"Hey bud. I think I meditated last night. I felt the Chi just by sitting and trying. I saw colors and felt the electricity. Only time was messed up. It felt like a minute or so but an hour must have passed. Am I imagining this stuff?"

Tommy brought over Brad's beer and cola.

"Beer and cola. You're a freak man!"

"You just don't know how to expand your horizons Tommy! Ha ha ha!"

"Freak!"

Tommy walked to the other end of the bar shaking his head and wiping off some of the surface of the bar between here and there with a sloppy wet rag that left a smear trail in it's wake.

Brad waited to reply looking at me and thinking. After a sip of his beer he said, "No, not imagining, it's real. What colors did you say you saw?"

"Purple, blue and hot vibrant pink." I replied.

"Interesting, very high frequency colors."

"I enjoyed the hot pink one the best, and when I came around it was like a jolt similar to waking after falling in a dream."

"Don't worry about it. It's perfectly normal. Yes you have learned how to meditate. The time thing is normal too. It's a great way to pass time quickly."

We talked some more about it and then went into discussions about work. After a couple beers we both left for home.

On August 6, 1997, a Wednesday, I left work early to pick up Sadie and the kids at the airport. The sun is bright and the air is clear with white puffy clouds as I view the downtown buildings on my approach from the east. What a good day to fly. They'll have a great view coming in.

I drove the car my wife had picked out for me in the used car lot on a snowy winter's day. We hadn't even test drove it before we bought it.

"This is the car!" She said. "It's the one you need to have. You'll love it."

It was out for a test drive with someone else by time we got to the point where she had talked me into trying it.

"Buy it without driving it!" she implored. "If you don't, it'll be gone when they return."

I made an offer for it. It was accepted and papers were signed before the other people trying it returned. As it turned out the people were upset as they did indeed want to buy it. They cleaned it up and we drove it home.

I was driving it now, thinking how right she had been. How did she know? The leather seats wrapped around me and the sound system filled my ears with joy. The smooth handling and quick response of the engine seemed an extension of myself. I didn't just drive this car, I was practically a part of it.

I could smell the jet fumes as I pulled into the airport. I remembered how good that had smelled when I returned from a trip to Korea. Somehow now though, they weren't quite as attractive. As usual I got a space to park in some 40 cars and a few rows or so from an entrance. I never did have much luck finding parking here.

I could feel the Chi as it rose through my feet and hands in the terminal. Is this an energy center? Here in an airport? "Why not?" I thought. A lot of people pass through here.

I checked the video monitor and found the arrival gate. At the gate the monitor said the flight was "delayed". Well, I was twenty minutes early already. How much longer would it be?

I sat in one of the chairs not really noticing anyone and thought maybe I could meditate to pass the time. I thought I'd do it for half an hour. I sat comfortably with my arms on the chair arms. I closed my eyes and felt my muscles relax all over. I felt the hum of the I-Chin energy and simulated some motions mentally to feel the imagined pull. I took some deep breaths then slowed my breathing to being barely perceptible. I could feel my pulse drop. I cleared all thoughts from my mind.

Shunk! I felt a snap into a different, uh, consciousness, I guess. Colors in my sight and energy filling me. I helped it along. The energy was very strong now, filling me up through my head, feet and hands and radiating out in all directions. My body was still yet it felt electric and light.

A New Reality

Shunk! Out of the colors and back into my seat. I opened my eyes slowly and the energy is still flowing. I look at my watch and see that a half an hour has passed within those few seconds of perception. I had come back at the exact time I had wanted to.

I stood to walk. The energy was still flooding through me and I felt very light. I hardly felt my footfalls in my boots as I walked. Everyone around me seemed to be glowing. I saw different colors surrounding their forms, traveling with them in an outline around their bodies. Some outlines were strong and radiated out a good distance. Others were tight and dull. I check the monitor. "Delayed" it said still. I walked back to my seat and watched everyone. It had to be, though I never even believed they existed before, Yes, of course, they were auras. I was seeing auras. "Hmmmm, Maybe I can sense what's going on with Sadie's flight," I thought.

I sat down again in the same position. This time I decided to come out of it only when they landed. Breathing down, heart rate down. Shunk! Into the colors. I see a face. Beautiful!! I don't know who it is and I can't tell if it's a woman or a man. I try to look closer and it disappears. "Okay", I think, "Sadie, find Sadie and the kids".

I see blue and white, just flashes of it. Could it be I'm seeing the clouds the plane is descending through? Could be. It leaves me quickly, or so it seems. I feel as if I'm in an elevator going down now. That sensation of dropping. Then it slows down and I feel a bump. Shunk! A jolt and my eyes open. Was the bump a landing?

I look at my watch and notice that twenty more minutes had passed. I was sure that bump was them landing. I go to check the display. "Arrived" reads the monitor. I go to the gate window and in a matter of a couple of minutes their jet rolls up to the gate.

Incredible! I actually felt them land (or so it seemed), I saw where they were but in that distorted time area. The twenty minutes felt like a few seconds, or a minute at most. Maybe that was why the descent seemed so rapid in my mind.

The energy was less now but still there.

"Hi guys!" I called as my brood approached. We spoke about the flight and Sadie told me about the delays as we hugged and kissed one another and left for home.

I continued to practice the meditation throughout the month whenever I had the time to. Whether it was on the beach, or on the back deck, or in the recroom. Music seemed to have an effect on it as it seemed to act as a focusing media. It would concentrate my thoughts on the sounds of the music which would drown out the other noises, such as the television, when I was in the recroom. On the beach, or on the deck, as well, it was able to drown out the external distractions well enough to be able to get that "Shunk" snapping feeling when I went into that other realm.

I assumed the realm was another type of consciousness at some other level of being. The fact that time seemed out of relation, to the regular passage of it, fit with the way I would perceive things occurring in the regular realm when I was in the altered realm. For example, the passage of the clouds and sky being viewed as flashes.

If I was in a realm where the time was passing at a much faster rate, it would make sense that the perceptions I had of the place where the time was slower would occur in flashes, kind of like a time lapse video. Since I was proceeding through at a higher rate I could only grasp instants versus a continuum, kind of like looking out the side window of a car going at a high rate of speed and blinking rapidly. Or, as another example, the effect of a strobe light. Thus, it would seem that not being in synchronous alignment with the passage of time would give that sort of viewing. Of course there was also the thought that I could be going insane or having some sort of a nervous breakdown. That would probably be the answer of choice from most.

"There I go again," I thought, the engineer in me trying to make sense of this marvelous gift (burden?, insanity?) opening before me rather than trying to just accept it. But I guess that's the way I am. If it doesn't make sense, then I have a hard time believing it, so the logical portion of me goes to work to find the reasons for it. For now, I guess that is an acceptable theory for me. But auras? I worried a bit about me. Only kooks see, or say they see, auras….right?

Once we got back home, and settled, the kids went off to do their thing, happy to have returned. Finally, I had the chance to talk with Sadie.

"Well I'm glad you guys are back. It's been a long week. Lots of weird stuff going on."

I looked back at the kids then at Sadie again. I grabbed Sadie's hand and squeezed it and she squeezed it back. We went into

24

the recroom where we were alone. I filled Sadie in on my strange experiences.

"That's how the week went, all this energy stuff. And at the airport when you were delayed, I went into a meditation, which by the way I didn't know it was when it first happened but Brad told me that's what it was. But anyway, I asked that I be brought out when you landed. Then I asked to go to you and I saw flashes of white and blue, like the clouds as you were landing, but it was as if a strobe light was on it. Just flashes, ya know? Then I felt a thump and I knew you had landed. I went to the monitor and it said , "arrived" and you showed up at the gate a few minutes later after taxiing. Another thing that happened was that when I came out of it, it felt like I was floating and not walking, and everyone had these colors around them. I rubbed my eyes but it wouldn't go away. Then after a bit it faded."

Sadie looked at me with concern on her face.

"Maybe you need a vacation, hun. You've been working really hard, ya know?" "That's got nothing to do with it. I tell you something has changed in me. For the better, I hope. I have to find out what's going on with this. I'm sure it's happened before. There should be something in books and stuff, and Brad says it's normal."

"Oh good, that makes me feel good, Brad thinks it's okay? Brad is a bit weird, don't you think?"

"That's just because he has such a high IQ. People like him seem weird to everyone. An IQ of 185 is a bit more than most people have. They say you need to be within 35 points of someone to understand them or, to communicate well with them."

"By the way, I have a meeting in PA coming up, for a whole week. I have to present some stuff and there will be about 125 people there from around the world. It's a sharing of info meeting for the group."

Sadie looked at me shaking her head, "Just what you need. To be gone for a week and buried again when you get back and still no vacation."

"I have to go. It's a political thing, if I'm not there it looks bad since we have the largest division. I already tried to get out of it."

Sadie gave me a look as if I were a sick puppy as she put her hand on my leg as we sat on the couch.

"Well hold it together for me, okay? You're starting to worry me." She kissed me on the cheek.

I continued to meditate occasionally, but that continues through the thread of time of this story. As it has interest to the tale, I will elaborate on the instance. However, other things besides meditation and resulting experiences were occurring. The reasons for them were still unclear but later reveal themselves. One such instance was an unusual delivery of myself, and a friend, to a place I never would have gone to on my own.

Our Lady Of Lourdes

It was now August 28, 1997. A pleasant warm day with the sun shining and not too much humidity. Tom, the Plant Engineer, and I had completed our morning walk when I was paged by the General Managers secretary. I answered the page from the plant.

"Yeah Missy, this is A.J. . . . What's up?"

"You need to get these boxes of wine from all the plants over to the country club where Ron's retirement party is going to be."

"Me? Can I assign it to someone or does it have to be me?"

"It has to be you. I don't know why but Donnie told me to have you do it. Anytime before the party will be fine. You don't have to do it right away."

"Okay, I'll probably get to it after lunch. See ya later Missy."

I went about my other tasks of following up on the problems Tom and I had found in the morning and problems that still existed from previous days. I did my voice mail, e-mail and paper mail, approved requisitions for items needed by the plant or engineering. When I saw Tom again it was almost lunch time.

"Hey, we have an important assignment buddy!" I jabbed at him.

A New Reality

"What do you mean **we**?! Do you have a mouse in your pocket or something?"

"Donnie wants me to drop off all those wines from the plants for the Presidents' retirement party. Since I have to do it I figured you could go too and we could get a look at the new Corporate Headquarters on the way back. Besides, you know where the country club is and I don't."

"Yeah, I guess that sounds like a good idea. I've been wanting to see the new headquarters anyway."

We went to lunch and got our home cooked meal at the local bar/restaurant. Along with the great food we always got our hugs and kisses from the owner's wife and her daughter. The place was very friendly, obviously, and the people were wonderful. The family did it all together and had a very successful business going. We took advantage of the food and the love daily.

After lunch we got back to work and loaded the car up with all the wines. They were local wines from the areas where each of our plants were located. The President liked sampling wines so this was a fitting gift to remember the plants by.

We drove off and delivered the wines. We dropped them off in the extremely well kept, upscale, old fashioned, country club. I felt totally out of place in this foreign place where the rich went to relax and do business on the grounds. When we were done we attempted to find our way to Corporate Headquarters. Tom knew the area fairly well and we thought it would be a simple thing to do. That is, until Tom said,

28

"Oh shit! How did we get here? We're way off base from our target now. This is where I grew up as a kid. I used to ride my bike on these streets!"

"Do you know where we are?"

"Of course, I just don't know how we ended up here. Just go straight and we can go back to the plant. We're too far from Corporate to try for it now."

Tom started to reminisce about the old days and told some stories about those days. He identified the streets and what things looked like back then. Pretty soon we were passing a place he remembered very well.

"Oh my God! That's Our Lady of Lourdes. I haven't been there in years. My grandmother used to take me there all the time. It's a beautiful place. I need to go there sometime. I had forgotten all about it! Hey, what are ya doin?"

"I'm turning around and going there. It'll only take a few minutes. Maybe this is why we got sent on this stupid mission. Seems kind of strange how we ended up here."

"Okay, I'm game. I can't wait to see the place."

We pulled in to the parking lot and I immediately started to feel some kind of energy. Naturally I didn't say anything to Tom. We got out of the car and started walking up a path as Tom said he remembered this or that. The closer we got to whatever was ahead the stronger the Chi was through my feet and hands. By time we got to the end I was flowing with it.

A New Reality

The end was an outdoor church and there were about a hundred people there. They were saying the rosary together. It sounded like an ancient ritual chanting. We sat down on a bench in the back and I looked at Tom. He was visibly disturbed in some way.

I whispered to him, "What's up?"

"Shh!" he said.

I listened to the chanting and felt the energy there. I need to come back here myself I thought. I never felt this energy when I had gone to any other church before. Of course when I had gone to other churches before, I had never felt this energy yet either. But, maybe something special *was* here. When Tom was ready, we stood and started to walk back to the car. As soon as we were a comfortable distance from the crowd, so as not to disturb them, Tom told me what had happened. He had heard voices and had felt something he couldn't describe.

"Wow! That was incredible!" he cried. "I never experienced anything like that. It felt powerful. I don't get it. Anyway, did you know that they say this is a healing place? It has a stone from the Lady of Lourdes in France and people come here from all over to be healed. I guessed this was my lead to start talking about this stuff to him. I spoke of the energy and what I had felt there as we drove back to work. The energy was starting to dissipate now but I could still feel it slightly. I told Tom what I had felt there but that it wasn't the first time I had felt it. Tom didn't know what to make of all of it. I think I made him pretty uncomfortable talking about it too. Most people don't like to think about this stuff too much. All I knew was I would be going back there someday although I didn't know why.

I didn't know a lot of things. My grandfather used to say to my dad, and my dad would quote him to me as I do to my children and my friends as follows:

"You spend your life learning and then you die a dummy."

Rather simple, but how many times I have felt this way is beyond counting. You could learn forever and still have more to learn. I had quoted under my picture in the high school yearbook a line from a popular song at the time. I never realized how well it would apply to me in later years. The line was, "Thinking is the best way to travel." I never thought the mind would be able to take me on the journeys it presently was, or was going to. If it was the thing we called, the "mind."

I had seen a show on television on one of the educational channels and it seems fitting to describe it a bit here. The show was about quantum physics. It tried to explain the subject in layman's terms. I myself had never studied physics to this degree, just regular run of the mill physics with $E=MC^2$, F=MA and all that four dimensional physics. Now the quantum physicists took everything a bit further. The elite of the physics community went to great lengths to extrapolate extra dimensions beyond our normal four (length, width, height, and time). They came up with there being eleven mathematically provable dimensions (length, width, height, time, and seven more). They also added that there may be more, but they hadn't been able to get there yet. There is a wealth of literature on this subject today written by some of the sharpest thinkers alive. I have listed a number of books on it in the bibliography at the end of this book.

Well, you ask, that's all well and good but what the heck does that have to do with the subject at hand!? I guess in my "normal", rational, logical method of deducing and trying to understand things, I felt this was very similar to the situation at hand. The reason being the way they described our perception of all these additional dimensions and my current perception of these happenings.

As everyone knows we live in a ***perceived*** four dimensional world. The four dimensions being defined as: length, width, height, and time. Length, width and height giving us our three dimensional shapes in the world and time giving us a dimension in which to move the shapes through (physics in four dimensions). Thus, with time there can be velocity and acceleration and corresponding forces generated, which can move these objects within these three other dimensions. These are all given, and automatically occurring daily **without question** by us, in our environment. So much so, as to be taken for granted, due to the lack of thought required for their occurrence. Without time there can be no motion. What would be missing if the other proven dimensions weren't there? Hmm.

Now the show demonstrated the truth to my grandfathers saying. Here is where they showed a man living on a piece of paper. A stick man drawn on a piece of paper living on the two dimensional plane of the paper with time as his *third* dimension as opposed to our fourth. He goes about life happily existing in his little world, until that is, something happens which he can't conceive of, never mind explain. The silly joker who lives in the four dimensional world (ours) decides to take a pencil and shove it through the piece of paper next to the happy two dimensional man. "Yikes!" yelps the two dimensional man as he can perceive the rip in the fabric of his plane (paper) but he has no clue how it got there, what caused it and if it will happen again! He can't perceive the added dimension we live in so thus he can't explain it. What will he do? He will try some way to rationalize this occurrence based on his current perceptions. When he can't rationalize it, maybe he'll call the thing that made the hole a "God" or something.

Well, here we are now, and the darn quantum physics guys "PROVE"[1], by means of their mathematical dexterity, the undeniable fact that at least eleven dimensions exist. Well, I have to tell you, I certainly cannot perceive of eleven dimensions. I can't even think of what the one past time is. Mathematically, they exist. We can't perceive it.

Now I **perceived** something **I can't PROVE.** This is the inverse of being able to **prove** something that **can't be perceived** as the eleven dimensions are. Is that something that I perceive real? I certainly must say it *feels* real. As time goes on I believe more and more it is real. Is it a "God" thing? I have to say yes due to the paradigms I'd been raised with, but probably the two dimensional man does too (depending on how he was raised of course). But eleven dimensions? All I know is there is so much we don't know.

Why reject anything that causes no harm and only can help? From fear maybe, but why reject things from fear. Fear can be totally unjustifiable at times. Worry demonstrates this point well. Phobias do too! Not to mention everyone's normal fear of the unknown, of change, or of straying from the existing beliefs they had been given.

I choose to learn all I can from this life. Do you? You may close your mind to the unknown for fear it won't "fit" your "beliefs" you call knowledge, or your present knowledge from sources unquestionable in your mind. I think you will agree, life is for learning or you would not have picked up this book and gotten this far in it. The world never did really turn out to be flat did it even though a round earth was in conflict with the current beliefs of the past. We aren't the center of the universe either as believed then.

So, in the words of a very smart man whom I respect for his hard work, wisdom and care for his family, "You live your life learning then you die a dummy."

A.J. Aaron

Pink Monkey

"Great spirits have always found violent opposition from mediocrities. The latter cannot understand it when a man does not thoughtlessly submit to hereditary prejudices but honestly and courageously uses his intelligence."
— Albert Einstein

I saw Brad in the usual place at the coffee machine early one morning, he seemed to know I needed to speak with him once more. I put the change in the machine and he nodded and selected his coffee and we stood as he watched the cup fill. He nodded at the door and we walked outside. After the door shut he looked at me through his thick glasses, sipping his coffee as he waited for me to begin.

"Well bud. The world seems to get less and less familiar to me. It seems your exercises have put me into a new world view."

"Not just the exercises. They can help you though. You were ready is what it was. This is happening to many now, more and more."

"Can't be. That means they must all be going nuts like me."

Brad laughed now as he crumpled up his coffee cup.

"Ha ha ha yea, some more than others."

"How do you know so much about this?"

"It's everywhere, the answers are that is, once we choose to listen and allow our paradigms to be released. It's actually remembering what we already knew but had forgotten, or been taught to not believe.

"Would I be wrong to say you aren't normal. I mean, more so than just the I.Q. and the way you act. No offense. It just seems you are "other worldly" in some way."

"Ha ha ha, not normal. That's a compliment to me. As far as other-worldly, well, sometimes I feel that way. Kind of like a pink monkey."

"Pink monkey?"

"Yea, you never heard of that term? There was a study done about social behavior. A group of PhD's dyed a monkey pink and, to be sure, they had a controlled variable, another monkey was dyed, but his normal color. They stuck them back in with the rest of their group. Before he was pink he was well accepted in this social group."

"What happened after?"

"They tore him to shreds, in a matter of minutes. He was different from the group after he was pink. Moral of the story, if you become different from the group, and you are, don't let them know. Or, at least try to look like them."

"What's that got to do with my question?"

"Sorry, allow me. You are becoming a pink monkey as I already am. Don't let others know too much about how pink you are. Their fears will destroy you. He who believes needs no explanation. He who does not will find no explanation that is sufficient. Don't let them try to explain you to themselves. They won't be able to, and fear, and the resultant rejection of you, will result."

"I needed that story?"

"Yes. Don't ever forget it."

"So what about you. Is that all that can define your difference?"

"I have come to find my purpose is basically to act as a catalyst. You know, like in chemistry. I speed up reactions. I make change come about more quickly. I won't be here much longer though I'd like to stay. It never seems to work that way. "I have other places to go other people to speed along their path. So I hear you're going out of town in a bit?"

"Yea. A week in P.A."

"For what purpose are you going?"

"Political mainly, though the purpose is to share information with the rest of the divisions."

"Pay attention. You're going for a reason. Answers are there. Your path requires you go."

"Don't start that shit Brad. More mumbo jumbo."

"K boss. You will gain insight this trip and not only from the meeting. Travel safe. Keep an open mind."

Work and the Plateau

The month of September wasn't unlike the many months before. Hectic, making little headway at true change, not a lot of fun. We laid people off then recalled them three weeks later. Needless to say this type of environment becomes a C.Y.A. environment quickly. There weren't a lot of people having fun anymore, and what had been built was now being destroyed.

Tom and I were two who felt it greatly since we had been there for over eighteen years now. We were part of the team that created what existed; a money making machine that created not just a return to the shareholders, but lives for people. The machine went from a two percent return on assets to a sixteen percent return under our old GM's reign. An improvement of 8 times! It would take a while to destroy this since it had taken all those years to build it. It could be done though. That was our deepest concern. It seemed to be happening already. Then what would become of those lives that were being created?

Maybe this was my testing ground and maybe soon I'd be able to be released from these tests and let someone else play this game. It didn't seem that it was always this way but lately it was. Don't get me wrong, this company was outstanding compared to many but there were times when these types of tests occurred to make people better, intended or not.

When you are raised in an organization by a man who not only knew the business from the supervisory level to his now very lofty corporate position, but who knew all the people and was a trusting and trustworthy individual, you notice the difference. This man had a charismatic personality and a strong sense of direction as to where we were going. He didn't put much stock in things like personality profiles and psychological tests. Not because they weren't necessarily useful but because he knew the people better than the tests could reveal.

He could tell more about a person from a single conversation than any personality profile could reveal. He had tremendous instincts and intuition. He was one of the youngest ever, upper level, managers in the corporation. At the age of thirty one he became the G.M. I was the youngest Plant Manager at the time at the age of 31. This guy was the General Manager over all the plants and the whole unit at that age. He quickly built the division up to 1300 people and two hundred million dollars in sales. As I said earlier, profits increased and the Board of Directors and the Corporate Management were thrilled. He used to say we were bringing big bags of cash and throwing them on the table for the corporation to use for growth.

Somehow though, I knew it wouldn't be long before a change occurred. I had been having this recurring dream about trying to climb a plateau. Initially, I didn't recognize it as recurring, until one morning I remembered it vividly and knew I had been having this dream for some time now.

The plateau was a rock of great proportions. The edges were steep and all of the surfaces were wet. I saw a small, gentle and friendly figure at the top waiting for me to climb up. It seemed they

knew me though I didn't recognize them. Try as I may I just kept
slipping due to the fact that it had just rained earlier and the surfaces
were wet. I tried to go up it in my four-wheel drive, primer gray,
pickup truck (which I never had possession of except in this dream)
but still no luck.

I then saw a house nearby where the roof was at the same
level as the plateau. It appeared that if I could get to the roof of that
house I might be able to jump across to the plateau. Yes, a shortcut, I
thought.

I went inside the house and there were a number of people
leaving and arriving. I worked my way to the top floor. As I tried to
cross the floor to the side where the plateau was, I'd keep falling
through the floor. I'd catch myself at my elbows and pull myself
back out. The ceiling below now had holes in it from me, and from
others, trying to do the same thing. Every time I fell through, my
wife was standing there by my side. She didn't help me at all, but she
was always there observing. Finally after many struggles I gave up
and found my way back down.

That day I started to tell my friend Tom about the dream and
what it seemed to represent started to become clear to me. The
plateau was a higher level of achievement of some sort and there
were people already there. One of them was a yet unknown friend of
mine and was waiting for me to arrive. Many other people were
trying to get there as well. My wife wouldn't help me get there, but
she would stay and observe passively as I struggled. The object of

trying to get to the plateau from the roof was to say, "There are no shortcuts." You must go directly up the slope.

How did I ever come up with this analysis? This is pretty weird, for a logic wired dude, as this is all an intuitive sort of extrapolation that my mind just made! Yow!

Insanity aside, applying logic to this intuitive conclusion I thought, "How was I to get there then!?" I couldn't climb it and I couldn't drive it. It was too slippery. Then it hit me. The reason it was slippery was from the rain. The rain had now stopped and all I had to do was wait. If I waited until it was dry, I would be able to ascend the slope without any difficulty.

Could this be related to something at work? Was the rain actually stopped now? Would it dry and allow me to proceed? Was it related to things getting back to normal at work? Could this be related to my own personal growth. Who was the person at the top? I still had a lot of unanswered questions. I didn't know if they would ever be answered. My intuition was buying things my logic couldn't pay for!! SHIT!

Yes, confusion at work and a tense environment without a good vision of where we were going. Me, a Plant Manager responsible for the livelihood of 250 people, in the midst of this nightmare, and I now end up having dreams and seeing auras and feeling energy fields. A good combination to put someone over the deep end. Well, at least one thing was for certain about that dream. My wife would stay beside me while I got through all this.

A New Reality

So I continued my day to day torture. I went to the grievance meetings. I held three shift meetings for United Way with everyone in the plant. I gave customers and company people, from around the world, tours of the facilities and its personnel and advanced processes. I constantly filled my daily planner up to the point where I practically had to plan a time to go to the bathroom.

The month flew by with little enjoyment and little hope of change. To top it off I had to attend a weeklong meeting out of state. It was a worldwide meeting; manufacturing managers, plant managers and engineers and hourly personnel were there from around the world. Typically, everyone had to bring something for sharing knowledge with the rest of the group. It was a worthwhile meeting but extremely long and boring. A week was a long time to take out of a person's schedule. I wasn't looking forward to it. I had been told I would go though, even if I sent the engineers to make our presentation. We had to have a management presence there. The largest division in the corporation could not have a Plant Manager not show up, or there would be a political problem. If that happened it would appear there was a lack of support for the program in other's perceptions.

So, I went. The meeting that occurred though wasn't what I had expected. It was probably one of the most important meetings in my life as well, though the true meeting had nothing to do with work. Brad was right when he told me it would be. Off to Pennsylvania.

Beth Terras

Unknown to me, in a house in Pennsylvania, was a person having a birthday. A birthday on the same day I was going to the meeting in Pennsylvania. A person by the name of Beth Terras, whom I would soon meet.

The house was typical of the houses built in the area. The row houses nestled close to one another as if to protect each other, from rolling, or sliding, down the steep hills. Protect from the driving winds that bring the deep snow. Protect their occupants with their stately height resisting the winds of change. On the front steps of almost all of these houses was a potted plant or two. The sidewalks were clean and swept. A cat sat on one stoop, a lazy dog on another. Someone had left a package of banana bread wrapped in tin foil on one stair maybe for the mailman, or the occupant, to arrive. Though the houses made good use of the front width to fit them all together, the back yards were deep, and full of flowers on every edge of the deep green grass. The houses reminded one of the friendliness and neighborliness of the past when they were built and filled with immigrants. Inside one of these houses it was someone's birthday. Isn't it always *someone's* birthday? Of course, but not always *this* someone's birthday.

"Jay, Thanks for remembering my birthday!" Beth said as she sat on the couch against the wall while she leaned on an elbow on the arm of the chair. The home-made, afghan blanket draped over the back of the couch like a fine work of art. Beth was dangling her foot off the end of her long leg and swirling it in a circle while she smoked.

"Nine, twenty nine, fifty… not hard to remember Beth, no problem. I'm just glad your feeling good for it and things are going okay for you right now. You deserve much nicer for your birthday."

"Hey! I got it okay. I only need to take about a zillion pills a day and stick myself with needles, but heck, I ain't in no wheel chair and they aren't gonna get me in one!"

Beth's roommate, Jan, sat in the recliner across from Beth on the couch. She sat with her feet up as the music played on the stereo.

"Beth, so what do you attribute your well being too? The others you know that got MS like you are in wheelchairs and you aren't."

"Don't know. Guess I'm stubborn's all. Stubborn Irish! Shame I had to give up that job though. Used to love the travel and was pretty neat being the, Director of Finance. Now I'm just a momom. Damn! That was a long time ago!"

"I think breaking your back was probably a lucky thing. At least they finally figured out why you were having problems. Now ya won't be falling down in front of a bus or something anyway."

"You got a funny way of making bad things sound good! But yea, I guess things turned out okay. I can still dance and I plan on doing some of that this Wednesday."

Beth was looking at Jay, and the drum table in back of Jay, as she spoke. She motioned to that table on the other side of the room with all the birthday cards on it.

"Look at all those cards. I love getting cards. They make so many nice ones now. I got a lot of Angel cards this time too. They're so beautiful."

Jan turned to look at the cards and they all fell over. Not one against the other. Not a domino type of thing. Just fell.

"Damn what happened?" Beth looked at the clock in the entertainment center, it read 11:38.

Jan got up and went to stand them up again. They stood easily. She looked at the floor and found a feather.

"Your sister's up to things I'd say. Her Angel being was just here. Here's her calling card."

"A feather? We don't have any feather pillows. No down coats. Where can that have come from? Maybe you're right Jay. The doors aren't open. And you and I don't make *that much* breeze when we talk. Ha ha ha."

Beth looks at the clock again as the time flips from 11:38 to 11:39. Beth thinks, "Eleven thirty eight? Eleven thirty eight! Why do I care it's eleven thirty eight!"

"Hey Jan, ya know what?"

Jan comes over to Beth and lets the feather float down above her and goes back to her chair.

"What?"

"It's eleven thirty eight." Beth says as she holds her hand under the feather as it floats down.

"Yea so? What's that supposed to mean?"

"Exactly! What's that supposed to mean!? Ha ha ha." Beth laughs a deep heartfelt laugh, her musical voice resounding as she tickles herself with the feather and laughs some more.

"For some reason it seemed like I should remember that time. I had this feeling I had to look at the clock when the cards fell and so I did but I'll be DAMNED if I know why."

"Well then don't forget it!" I just hope you don't start remembering the time of everything happening around here. You'll just be *such* a fun person with all that information."

"Yea! Went pee at yadda yadda time, dropped dish at yadda yadda time, and cleaned the bathroom at yadda yadda time. I could tell you my whole day in riveting detail!! I do remember all the times of my kids births and weddings and all sorts of stuff. But why should I want to know this time?"

"Thanks but no thanks on those riveting details, but I think you got the time memorized when the cards fell okay. You can carry that time around for whatever reason it is, and I'm sure you will."

The Meeting

I was on my way out of state. The flight would only take about forty five minutes in the company jet. On board were myself, one of our hourly set up men, an engineer and my favorite boss, friend and leader, the President of our Group. The second from the top of the organization. The man who reported to the CEO. The man responsible for one third of the company. The man who had led our Division all those years through the tough times into the present. Can't you hear the, "Hail to the Chief" music now playing in your head? Ha ha ha. We used to sing that when he showed up at dinner, or at a night meeting. People would all look at us of course...., "Da dat da da dat de da de da de da da...."

As you can tell I had a lot of respect and love for this man. If he ever asked me to give him all my possessions and follow him I would do it in a <u>second</u>. Many people would. He's the kind of person that everyone implicitly trusted. I'd been locked out of his office by him before on several occasions but I always knew he wouldn't hold it against me and he appreciated the opinions of those working for him even though, as he said, "You get to voice your say but remember I'm the one who has to make the decision." I compare him to a John Kennedy or Hitler in his ability to have people want to follow him. I didn't get much opportunity to see him much anymore so I was happy to see him at the lobby of the jet's hangar.

"Hey chief!" I called out as I saw him in the lobby.

"Hi A.J. . How are ya!?"

"Hangin' in there Mike. Hangin' in there," I said as I shook his hand after we both looked around to see if we could get away with a hug here and knew we couldn't. Mike liked to use the old traditional European greeting for close friends when he could as did I. But to do it here would mess with the paradigms of acceptable behavior of the people around us now.

"You're presenting today?"

"Yes I am and I want to hear what you think about it after okay? This is a good group to go after with this. I don't get so many leaders assembled in one place like this."

"Everyone here?" called out our pilot as he grabbed my duffle bag and took it to the plane.

"Yup. We're ready if you are." I replied.

We boarded the seven passenger jet in the hangar then were pulled out to start the engines. Mike and I spoke some and I gave him a copy of a book I picked up at a one day seminar. I had it autographed to him. I knew it was something he'd enjoy since he was doing a lot of traveling and had worldwide responsibilities.

It was by Jack Naisbitt, "Megatrends Asia." The seminar was "High tech, High Touch" and covered a number of issues including the growing need for high touch things in society today to offset the high tech of e-mail and other touchless things. That is, the more technology we introduce, the more people have a need to be with people. Since Mike was a high touch type of boss this was another reason I knew he'd like the book.

We talked about the book a bit and he asked me to give it to him later, after his presentation. Then, after he handed out his notes, he would have enough room in his briefcase for it. Before we knew it we were landing.

I looked at my watch as we touched the wheels to the ground, and I noted the time, then calculated our total travel time. It had taken about thirty five minutes air time. What a way to travel. Going commercial takes 6 hours door to door due to no direct flights. This takes one and a half hours total, and no lines.

The ride to the hotel took about ten minutes. We checked in and rushed to lunch before the meeting began at one o'clock. We all ended up splitting up at lunch, due to the lag in check ins. It didn't matter much though. Everyone knew other people from the previous meetings. That was another advantage of these. It created a sense of community amongst the group and a feeling of reunion upon grouping together again.

The meeting started as usual with the Vice President of Manufacturing Services introducing the week's itinerary to the group and everyone then introduced themselves briefly to the group. Then it was time for Mike's presentation.

He had the rooms' attention quickly as usual. His charisma reaching out and touching each person. He went through the logical and intuitive sequence for implementation of the various techniques and methods of setup reduction, Kanban etc. Intuitive to him that is but not to everyone. The group had for years, at many locations, attempted to implement these strategies out of sequence with limited successes. Picking the things that were familiar or the easiest for them to implement. But as Einstein had said,

"If you want to create a logical and coherent system, do it by intuition." And that is what Mike did here by putting all the pieces together.

Mike was just about done with his presentation. The intuitive logic of it and its simplicity was being apparent now to the audience. The energy of the room was now feeling quite high with the questions being very much on target. It was at this time that the fire alarm went off in the room we were in and everyone started to exit as the hotel personnel came running in the room.

Nothing was wrong. There wasn't any excessive heat, nor was there any smoke, as this was a non smoking meeting. I met up with Mike on the way out.

"Damn, this happens everywhere I go these days," he said.

"I don't care if it's in Europe in a meeting, or at an airport. It seems wherever I am these damn alarms are going off."

"I think I can see why Mike." I said. "Your energy is so high it upsets the alarms."

"Ha, yeah, maybe!" He laughed and put his hand on my shoulder to send me through the doorway ahead of him.

His energy was high. It had been for years. He survived quite well on limited sleep and limited food. He would stay up late talking about work and life with whoever he was with. Building his popularity and gaining valuable insight as he went along. Now, the way I was feeling these things, I could actually feel it as it poured from him. I always joked with my wife that he was an Angel on this earth. Now I was beginning to believe it.

The rest of the meeting went on unremarkably for that day. We had a late dinner meeting and a presentation at dinner from some tooling suppliers. Afterwards, I had a beer with the old Plant Manager of my plant who had since been promoted. We had worked together for a couple of years when I had Manufacturing Engineering and he had the plant. It was always fun to get together.

That night I had the strangest dream. I woke from it about five AM. In my dream I was counting backwards through the alphabet letter by letter. As I arrived at a letter that was to be chosen I would feel an increase in the flow of electricity through me. The first letter I found was a "B". Then I started at "Z" again and went backwards. The next letter I found was an "E" It was at this point that my full body was feeling a tremendous rush flowing in waves from head to foot and back again. As I approached the next letter, the energy got unbearable....W,V,U,T.....It was so powerful it woke me and I sat there in wonderment of it. I tried to figure out what this meant but I didn't have a clue. "B and E and then I woke up at the "T". What was that supposed to mean? The energy was incredible. I laid there a while then got up for a shower and breakfast.

It was now Tuesday morning and the second day of the meetings. Some speakers kept you awake and others caused you to struggle to keep from hitting your head on the table. I would get up and get a coffee and stand for a while when it got bad. We had occasional breaks as well.

It was on one of these breaks that I noticed a very unusual painting in the hallway. I had returned my messages, finished my voice mail, and had sat down to enjoy a smoke and some coffee. I sat in this red leather chair opposite a particular painting many times before. I walked these halls for several years since this was where we had been having these meetings for some time now. I never once had noticed this painting before though.

I felt the flow of energy in me as I was sipping on my coffee. I looked up and noticed this painting in an ornate frame on the wall opposite me. It was a vase of flowers. The colors of the flowers were vivid and beautiful. So much so they seemed to just radiate energy of their own. It gave me a feeling like love and made my energy flow increase. I stood and walked toward it.

As I approached, the energy was strong. As I got very close, the vase holding the flowers in the painting showed a painful sight to me. It appeared to be that of an Angel that had been beaten down and was resting broken at the base. I couldn't see what had caused such an awful thing to occur to an Angel as the vase would need to be rotated to see the whole story. I could feel the pain there though. It was there with the energy and the love flowing from the flowers. Quite a contrast. All that love pouring forth from the flowers as the Angel writhed in agony beneath them, emanating its' pain. A startling painting. I'm surprised I never saw it before, though I felt it had always been there. Why did I perceive all this? I didn't know at the time but I later found out this was somewhat of a premonition of what was to come.

Since I now had come to like writing, I wrote a short story in several parts and posted it on the web. Over three thousand people had downloaded it and were following it. There was one of these three thousand though that enjoyed it thoroughly and would always ask for the next installment.

We had become friendly over time and knew about each others lives some and decided to meet if I ever got to the area. Well, I was in the area now, but I hadn't had a single communication from my friend as of yet. After the meetings were over, a group of us decided to go out to another Hotel where there was a DJ and an ongoing Trivia game being played. So I left a message at the desk for my friend on where I would be for the evening should they call or stop by.

We went to the other Hotel but it didn't take long for the group I was with to split up. Terry, the youngest of the group who was an engineer from Texas put it well for them.

"C'mon guys let's go. This is a geriatric convention here."

I wasn't about to go running about tonight. I had left a message where I'd be if my other friend arrived too, so I chimed in.

"You guys do what you want. Just remember to come back here and pick me up on the way home. I'm gonna just sit here and watch the crowd. Besides, it's early anyway and this crowd is probably from an insurance seminar or something. There's a DJ later and I'm sure there will be plenty of people to watch."

Seth and Fred joined in.

"I agree with A.J. . I'm gonna just relax here." said Seth.

"Me too." said Fred.

The three of us sat there as the others said their "See ya's"
and left.

"Remember to come back and get us!" I yelled as they were
leaving. Dave and Terry waved in acknowledgment. The waitress
came over and I ordered us another round of drinks. We sat and
talked about work. As we did the crowd was changing. The older
group was leaving bit by bit and being replaced by a younger group.
The mix was now leaning toward the twenty one to forty five year
old.

The DJ arrived and started to play some music. At that point
I decided to request some music and asked him to call out my
friends' name every now and then and ask that they go to the DJ's
booth. It was starting to get crowded and I didn't feel like constantly
searching the place. I gave him a tip and he did as I asked. It never
did do any good though. That friend had evidently never showed up.
It was as if the existence of that friend was just to have me stay put
tonight to meet this special person that I was meant to meet that I
wasn't aware of yet.

The music was now playing loudly yet no one was dancing.
Smoke is rising from a few of the tables. I can overhear some of the
conversations.

"Here we are again hun. I wonder if our lives will ever
change."

"I know, but think how long the week would be, well, this doesn't change it much, does it. What's the point?"

I watch as a man approaches their table.

"Hi, my name's Joe. I don't think I've seen you here before."

"Same old thing," I start to think to myself. All stuck in the loop. I'm talking with the guys at my table and then I feel as if someone is looking at me and turn my head toward them. I see a tall dark haired woman across the dance floor as she seems to feel me look at her and stops and looks back. As she does, I get another rush of the electricity and she hesitates, but continues, her journey across the floor. I sat back a minute in wonderment while the rest of our table chattered on. I lean back and close my eyes for a moment trying to focus on what just happened, or what it was that I imagined happened.

"Want another beer, A.J.?"

"Want another beer, A.J.? Hey!"

"Huh? Yea, sure, another beer would be good. Thanks bud."

Frank goes to get drinks for us and I look around. Realizing I now need to go to the bathroom, I lean over and tell Seth over the increasing volume of the DJ's music. I get up and move toward the men's room, maneuvering through the now, nearly full, nightclub.

I take care of business and wash my face and hands and comb my hair. As if the act of this would cleanse the confusion from me. I looked at my eyes in the mirror and seemed to get lost in them as if they weren't mine but someone else's. I splashed more water on my face and wiped it with a paper towel. Gosh, you'd think I had a ton of drinks and I haven't even had enough to get close to the legal limit. I must be going nuts.

I made my way back to my seat. As I passed by a dark corner on the way the energy starts again and I feel it getting stronger. I hesitated as the sound of the buzz happening was heard in my head and felt through my whole body. I moved ahead some more and noticed where the source of this increased energy is from. I saw a form in a dark corner of the room, as I got nearer to it, the energy increased. It's the woman I saw and connected to across the floor.

As I get closer I think to myself, "I need to speak with..."

I almost complete that thought in my mind and I now see her face clearly and she then answers me as if I actually said it!

"Yes, you need to speak with me. Have a seat."

We meet shaking hands and she smiles warmly. I look at her face and it's astoundingly familiar. Where had I seen that face before!

"My name is Beth Terras"

"I'm A.J. Aaron. What did you say your name was?"

"Nice to meet you Aej?"

"Same. What was your name?"

I was getting irritated by the loudness of the music. I guess the DJ was trying to wake people up when he turned it up earlier. I was straining to hear and raised my hand to my ear and leaned toward her. I looked at the DJ and thought how nice it would be if the volume went down a bit. The DJ looked back, stopped his conversation and headed back to his booth. The stranger now leans over and cups her hand along her mouth as she spells her name out for me into my ear.

"B.E.T.H!"

At that point I had a flash back to seeing those letters as she said each one. I see them the same way I did the other night when I counted backwards and got the first 3, "B.E.T.". The music gets quieter now.

"That's better," I say as I look back at the DJ again, "How did you know what I was thinking?" .

"I did? I just thought you wanted to speak with me that's all. Just a coincidence and a natural assumption, wouldn't you say?"

"I suppose. Gosh you look so familiar yet, I can't say why. Do you know me by chance? I mean we even exchanged first and last names. I feel as if we met before somewhere."

"I get that a lot. Some people used to say I looked like agent 99 on that old TV program Get Smart. Barbara Feldon was her name."

"That could be it and you do look like her a bit, especially in the lips and cheekbones, but that's not what I meant. I'm not sure what I meant. Familiar though. Very!"

As we spoke I could feel the interplay of energy between us. I think she did too. It was as if we we're joined somehow in this flow of electricity. I sat down at the tall bar seat at the opposite side of the small round table. We both gazed at each other silently for a while before we realized we were staring at each other.

As I stared at her, I nodded my head in acknowledgement of her not voiced question, then, I spoke as if I was answering a question Beth verbalized though she never did. I didn't even realize I was doing it at the time.

"From the Cleveland, Ohio area. I'm out here for a meeting till Thursday. God! You look so familiar to me but I can't tell from where. I don't recognize your name or your face, but the feeling of familiarity is overwhelming. The other feelings you give me are quite odd as well."

"Do you always answer questions before they're asked? You just answered everything I was thinking."

"I thought you asked. I guess you're right you didn't. I'm sorry."

"No need to be sorry. I think it was kind of interesting. To tell you the truth, when you came over I knew what you were going to say too, but it seemed so weird I tried to cover it up. I can tell you're not on the prowl, like some of the guys here, and not many people would say they need to speak with someone unless there was a problem or business issue. It's not a very friendly introductory remark. But there is something that you are confused about with me. How you're somehow drawn to me."

"Like a very intimate relationship. Very close… Can't remember."

"Yes! Lovers, husband and wife, parent and child, something."

Beth grasped my hand gently in hers and rubbed the top
with her thumb as if to garner more information this way. I hold it to
my face and close my eyes, trying to do the same.

"My god! I can't explain this feeling. I feel so close to you. It
can't just be love, can it? It's too intense! Why!? I don't even know
who you are."

"Yes, my body? soul? is feeling the same things, the rush of
an energy vibrating all over. It, it, feels like."

"Yes, a full body orgasm or something. Total bliss."

"Past lives? I never thought of that before. I suppose that
could be. Enough weird things have been happening lately that I
can't explain."

"Sure, Angel, I'd love to dance."

"Thanks. We gonna dance? I love to dance."

"Didn't you?.."

"No. Well I didn't say it. I don't think. Seems like I am. I
better watch what I think huh? Ha, ha, ha, ha."

We went to the dance floor and disappeared into our own
world. Light energy seemed to surround and dance about us joining
us together as one. Time stood still. I heard that saying before but
never experienced it. It was just us. We fit together like we'd known
each other forever. As the spot light would shine on her face as we
moved around the floor I knew where I'd seen her before. She
closed her eyes briefly and opened them to look at me then smiled
as the light illuminated her face. I saw that face before doing the
exact same thing. This was the face I saw meditating. In the

meditation it had appeared she was waking up. We go back to the table after a time.

"Where did you say you were from?"

"I'm from nearby, only a few minutes away. My daughter is here too."

"Your daughter is old enough to go to a bar?"

"She's old enough to have a son. I'm a mommom!"

"A What!?"

"Ha ha ha, a mommom.! Ha ha, a grandmother."

"No way. You're no grandmother! How old are you, if I may ask?"

"I'm forty seven. Born in 1950."

"Well, you sure don't look it. I thought you were much younger than that.

"Why thanks. I appreciate that. Are you sure your seeing the real me though? Ha, ha, ha. How old are you?"

"Forty."

"I thought you were in your early thirties myself. See how deceiving it is? I take care of my grandson and things like that. You see, I have Multiple Sclerosis, I was diagnosed at the age of 27. I had fallen down some stairs and broke my back when they found it."

I remember the picture on the wall with the Angel on it now. Its back was broken.

"I used to be the Director of Finance for a snack food company before that."

"Sorry to hear that Angel. You don't seem to have any problem with mobility though."

"Not too much now. Though I do have my times. I think a positive attitude helps a lot. My doctor likes me to talk to newly diagnosed patients as well, to help them. Sometimes it does get to me too though, but I try not to let it. It was real bad for a while but now I get by. Angel? You called me Angel again. Any reason? Why did you call me that? Not that I don't like it, but what made you say that?"

"I'm not sure. I guess it just fits. Something mystical and powerful about you. Full of love and very strong. That's the way you feel to me."

"Why thanks! You are so nice to me!"

Beth touches my hand with her fingers then reaches in her pocketbook and pulls out her keychain to show me the Angel. She lifts her coat off the back of the chair and shows the Angel on the lapel.

The broken Angel again came to my thoughts.

"You see, I collect Angels and my friends sometimes call me Angel because of it. My sister died at the age of 37. She's the reason I collect Angels, cause she promised me she'd watch over me as my Angel after she was gone.

"How did she die?"

"A brain aneurism. It was Thanksgiving. Like a few other deaths in my family. I don't like Thanksgiving much anymore."

"But I know my sister is with me all the time, or at least when I need her. She visited me the other day."

Now this strange woman was crossing the line of "normalcy", and I was feeling uncomfortable and beginning to think talking to her may have been a mistake. I looked at her face, still so familiar though. We seemed to fit so well as if we had known each other for ages already. I had a strange, powerful, knowledge of some type of connection to her. We seemed to know each other already. Her image that I'd seen in my mind before, the picture, the letters in the dream. I had to listen. I passed the fear by and put my attention back into the conversation.

"You okay?" She said as she looked at me with concern.

"Yea, yea, just thinking. Sorry. How did she do that?"

"Monday was my birthday, September 29th."

"Happy Birthday!"

"Thank you! Anyway, as I was saying, on Monday, Jan and I were sitting in the living room talking about things when all my birthday cards fell off the table onto the floor. It was as if a wind blew through the room but there wasn't any wind. No windows open. No one was walking by the table. They just fell. When I went to pick them up, there was a single white feather there. We don't have any feather pillows there. There was no reason for a feather to be there. I don't know where it came from. I looked at the clock when it happened and it was eleven thirty eight. I don't know why I remember that time, but I had to and I still do.

"What time was it?"

Now my mind is racing. I remember looking at my watch as we landed and noting the time when I figured out how long it took us. I could see my watch in my memory showing 11:38 as we hear the chirp of the jets wheels touching down and the roar of the reverse thrusters.

"It was eleven thirty eight. Why?"

"This was this Monday?"

"Yes, why?"

My heart was now racing as I tried to make sense of all of this. I felt like I was dreaming. This couldn't be real. I looked into BETH's smiling eyes studying them. Feeling her hand, feeling the energy, practically hearing the rush of it as it hums.

"Well Angel, I have a bit more to tell you about what has been happening the last couple of days. Let me start by saying that I think I was your birthday present. I think we were somehow meant to meet tonight, and somehow, we have something to learn or gain from each other. Let me tell you what's been happening. Our plane's wheels touched down on your birthday at eleven thirty eight, and the reason I stayed around here tonight was to meet someone who was a fan of my short stories, but they obviously haven't shown up. But now I think, ha ha well, I know, you're the reason I'm here. It started with a series of uh, dreams. I guess you'd call them that? Weird huh? Ready?

"Weird? Heck no!! I think my sister was watching out for me again. Go ahead and tell me about earlier this week. Now I know why I remembered that time. I'm listening."

A New Reality

The next morning I woke wondering what the day would bring and whether or not I was going totally insane. I ate breakfast and headed down to the meeting. I was exhausted but functional. I listened to the first presentation and during the second one, I received a smell of perfume to my nose. It was a familiar smell. I looked around the room.

The only women there were all the way across the room. I looked at the people next to me and they certainly weren't the source. I had changed clothes from last night and had showered so it couldn't be from me dancing with Beth. I tested myself and found nothing. I couldn't seem to smell it when I tried to with my nose. When I stopped trying it came back again. But it wasn't a smell, as I'd normally smell it. It was as if the smell originated in my brain directly. I could identify it now. It was the perfume Beth was wearing last night. Weird! Was I having a flash back memory? I was almost certain now I was going nuts! I was creating an illusion from a set of coincidences. I felt I was totally delusional.

I got up from my seat, went to the back of the room, got a cup of coffee, and snuck out the door to the hallway. I went down to the phones and found the slip of paper that Beth had written her name and number and address on. As I looked at it now, it seemed to be a fake. The number looked like something someone would make up. Especially if she was called "Angel". The number was 777-XXXX. I thought for sure that it would be a fake number so I figured I'd call it and get it out of my system so I could put this whole illusion behind me. I called.

"Hello?"

"Hi, this is A.J. . . I just smelled your perfume for some reason and then I thought I'd call and see if this number was real. 777? Odd."

"It's real, It's me all right. Smelled my perfume? Did you sleep okay? I thought you were leaving this morning."

"I am in a little bit. I had to be at the meeting at seven this morning not leave at seven. We take off about ten."

"Oh I see. Well thanks for the great conversation and dancing last night. It was real interesting. Best birthday present I ever got!"

"Thanks, me too. I think though it won't be the last time we're together."

"I don't think it will. Seems I know you so well already. Like I always have known you."

"Yea, well, I better get back to the meeting. Have a great day and I'll talk to you soon."

"Same to you…."

"See ya Angel!"

"Bye"

"Not Bye, that's too permanent…See Ya."

"K See ya A.J.. Ha ha ha"

I hung up the receiver. I went back to the meeting and left on the jet later that morning wondering what was really happening to me.

What To Do Now?

We were on the jet and ready to take off. Kevin, a guy from corporate who helped conduct this meeting, asked me for a pen. I looked for mine and couldn't find it. I gave him my pencil instead.

"Here Kevin, I can't seem to find my pen right now."

"You're kidding me. The one that Ron gave you about a million years ago that you showed him you still had? The one he gave you for bringing your division to first place in the Corporation at cost reduction? The one that you said you never lose?"

"That's the one. The one I said always shows back up."

"Well I hope it does this time."

"It hasn't missed yet. I'm sure it will."

Sure enough, I had lost it. I wasn't quite sure where but it must have been at the nightclub last night. If I did, I don't know how it will turn up now. But somehow, I knew it would.

The flight was uneventful. When we landed, I decided to go straight home since I had been gone all week. I thought a lot about what had happened. My analytical self was not very comfortable with all of this. I wasn't feeling any energy now and was pretty relieved that I didn't at this point. On the ride home, as I approached the mall, I had to detour because of construction. I wasn't planning on going to the mall but the detour through the parking lot led me right where I would have gone, the record shop. I thought, "Okay, if there is a parking space right in front, I'll stop, and if not I'll keep going."

There was a spot right in front. The closest spot to the door beside the handicapped spots, of course. I parked the car and stepped into the heat of the day. I pulled my wallet from my pocket as I entered the store.

"May I help you?' The girl asked as I entered the store.

"No, but thanks anyway. I have some albums to look up." She nodded her head and smiled as she left me to go on my search. I took out the note with the albums listed from talking with Beth last night. I walked over to the computer and searched for the album. It told me the section it was in and that it was in stock. I searched the rest. They were all in the same area and were in stock. I walked over to the section the computer told me they were in. As I pulled each one from its location, I looked at it briefly then put it back down. None of them seemed to attract me, except one. It was "Kitaro's" Dream. I could feel it pull me somehow. I didn't hesitate as I took it to the counter and purchased it.

When I arrived home I pulled into the garage and unloaded the car, dragging my luggage and briefcase into the house.

I unloaded my luggage and briefcase and dragged my things into the house.

"I'm home!" I cried out.

"Hi papa!" my son said as he played his video game as I entered the house through the recroom.

"Hi buddy," I returned, touching his head as he sat on the floor in front of the TV.

A New Reality

"How's things goin?' I asked. He kept at the game as he said, "Okay!"

I went up the stairs, kissed Sadie as she gave me her cheek to do so. I found Kara in the playroom and did the same. I emptied my bag from the trip and discussed the events of the past few days with my family over dinner. I didn't include my strange encounters since the kids were there and I wasn't sure how Sadie was going to react. After supper I went out to the front yard to have my coffee and listen to the new CD.

As it turned out the CD had quite an impact on me. It turned out to have Jon Anderson in it as well as Kitaro. I never knew he did any work with them. It was an intriguing, emotional album. There was one song on it in particular that caught my interest and pulled at my heartstrings. It felt as if someone had died and the artist was writing a requiem about him or her. Yet there was lightness to it. I tried to listen to it over and over but couldn't due to the pain it elicited in me.

Why did I feel such emotion from a song? Yes, that is what music is meant to do but not to me. I was an engineer, a logical and emotionally level person who doesn't feel all that much. The cool headed, seldom-angered, seldom-jubilant, seldom-sad person was feeling all this emotion from the song. Hmmmm. I'd have to work on that one. Music can put me in a mood but this was a feeling of severe loss that I felt from it.

There was another song though that told its own story immediately. It also applied to the recent meeting I had with this stranger. Or did it helped to explain it? I still wasn't sure. The title of the song was "Agreement". Some of the lyrics from it are as follows:

"Watching the world

From our window of life

Can we see all there is

That is real

That is right

To the distance so far

From our true understanding

Making us want more

Making us see less….."

And it continues

"The fire within your eyes

This mystic time

I've known before

Once before

The flame within my heart

Agreements made

Are now realized

Like before

Agreements of Trust

Agreements of Faith

Agreements of Truth

Agreements of Liberty"

A New Reality

Could it be that what Jon Anderson was singing was the state I was currently in? I know it felt that way. Could it be possible to have made agreements in another life to meet another person in this life? Could it be possible? Is there more than one life we live? Could it be, that all those coincidences that occurred, were for a reason and for real? If so, what were the reasons? Could this woman and I be connected in some way from a past life if such a thing could possibly exist? This was getting a bit crazy; finding this album at this time, with this bit of information. Maybe she chose this album as a plant for me to come to this conclusion. But what of the song without words that had those deep felt emotions associated with it that I couldn't explain. I needed to analyze that song more.

I tried time after time to listen to it in full but the power of it was such that it would pain me to hear it. I felt much the same as if someone or something I loved had died. When I looked up the cut number I read the title, "A Passage of Life." Needless to say they had done an excellent job of representing that aspect. I continued to try to listen to it till I was finally able to get through it all and listen deeply to it. I let it tell me its story, so to speak, as I felt it through. Then finally on October 9, 1997 I realized what it was and why it affected me so deeply. The thoughts I recorded that day in my journal are as follows:

"Initially I felt it was about death as my first impressions had told me before I had even read the title. It isn't about death per se though. It gave me fear and sadness, which I interpreted as death of a friend. It is in a way but not literally. In actuality what it conveyed to me was the death I thought I would have at the age of 35.

When I was younger I thought I would die at the age of thirty-five. Why I thought that was beyond me but I never truly let go of that thought though I was past thirty-five. I knew if I was to be king, as I longed to do, I would need to do it by then. Well, I did become king, so to speak, in my accomplishment of becoming a Plant Manager of a fortune five hundred plant doing 26 million dollars in sales at the age of thirty-one. I was now forty and still alive though. As I listened to the music now, I knew somehow the real meaning of those pre cognitive projections of death at thirty-five, or, whatever they were, that told me those things.

It is the transformation into the true self that was to occur. The "new you", if you will. The melancholy is the passing of the old self never to be returned. But there is a power and lightness to the song as well. That was the feeling of the new self. No longer encumbered by fear and prejudice, or concern over other peoples perceptions of me, or whether or not I am working hard enough, or making everyone happy. I would no longer be encumbered by all those fears and preconceived notions and paradigms of how to live. It is in the realization that life is love and fear is useless. It is the death of the old me and the formation of the new me.

The sadness comes from knowing that all the things that were so important before (i.e., What people thought, money, being right, being better than everyone else, etc.) are all things of the past and hold little, real value. Sadness to know that all those things that were thought to be important to living a good life were not the **least** bit important. Finally, achieving a realization that the fullness of life is now here and the thing that was perceived as life so far, for so long, was simply an illusion to demonstrate the problems and get me to the here and now.

There is sadness knowing my life will never be the same again. The good and light part of the music is that it will be a wonderful life ahead full of love and abundance. This you can bet on. The love is now within. The pain of the struggle to get there is over. The joy of the future is laid before me to consume, and contribute to, for eternity, never having to relive my errors. I have started to grow now to the levels of life humans were meant to grow to. Fear no more!

There is more to life than trying to be better than someone else or trying to satisfy everyone in achieving *their* view of what success is. The mystery of life unfolds as a flower in the breaking day. The cold mist of the evening going away in the warmth of the morning sun as the flower opens to the light, a light that has been there before, but seems to be the first time in its newness."

This process of figuring out what that song was about and how it related to me took a few days of listening. The conclusion I came to was something that I previously would never have come to. Heck I never would feel any emotion like that from a song! My mental problems must be getting worse I thought. Yet it had flowed fluidly from my pen to the page of the journal, each time I sat and listened. Now I'll tell you how my wife reacted to my meeting on the night I had gotten home from it.

The kids had gone to bed and Sadie and I were sitting on the loveseat in the recroom watching TV. The comfort of being home again wrapped me in peace while the thought of what Sadie will say wracked my nerves. I wasn't one to hide anything and couldn't lie. I had to tell her as soon as possible or I would go crazy. I looked at her as she sat there in her usual relaxed state. She was the reflection of a still pond with no ripples.

"Sadie, I have to tell you a story. You might think I'm crazy but it's all very real to me. Don't worry I'm not going to quit my job or run away somewhere. It has to do with some strange happenings that occurred. It has to do with the Chi I felt before when I was doing the I-Chin exercises and then while meditating and when you were returning from Florida and I saw and felt you guys landing and the Auras and all of that."

"I don't think you're crazy."

"No?"

"I don't know what to make of it but I've heard of those things happening to people. I don't think you're crazy."

"Well, that's a good start but let me tell you about the trip this past week."

I went through the whole story as she sat patiently and looked into my eyes. The dream, the fan of my stories that I was trying to find, the painting, and the meeting. When I was done I told her the woman wasn't a threat to our relationship in any way but I knew she would be my friend for the rest of this learning stage. I felt like I knew her forever yet we had only spent a few hours talking. When I was done I asked my wife if this bothered her.

"How do you think I feel? How would you feel if I came home and I told you I met a man I was going to be a friend with?"

"I don't know. I'm not in that position and after this I would probably understand it pretty well. You know I didn't have to tell you but I couldn't do that and like I said it doesn't change our relationship at all. I still love you. I am still committed to our marriage. I am not having sex with this woman nor did I. The thought never entered my mind nor do I ever intend to."

"Well I guess men can have woman friends but this does seem strange."

I could tell that Sadie wasn't comfortable but the worst was over at least. I knew she would accept this eventually and in time she did. Beth and I corresponded and spoke on the phone with some regularity. I showed Sadie the letters we wrote back and forth and the pictures she sent. (By the way, my pen had fallen into Beth's pocket book that night in PA.. and she sent it back in the first mailing. The pen I had never lost before. If I hadn't called her the first time she would have ended up contacting me anyway via mail or phone due to the pen. Coincidence? Maybe. Did she keep it as an excuse to contact me if we didn't stay in touch? Maybe again but I doubt it.) Sadie and Beth spoke on the phone a few times. We sent books and music back and forth across the miles. But there was more happening here than just a new friendship. There was something that made this relationship entirely different than any other I had experienced until then. Somehow, we were connected.

We would literally feel each other from time to time and were able to tell what the other was feeling and somewhat of where they were. The connection at times was constant and almost annoying. It was as if there was an open channel between us. There was constant input from outside of my normal five senses.

One such time I was sitting in the love seat watching television in the recroom with the family. As I sat there, I got a rush of that same energy sensation. I immediately recognized it as Beth, and it felt overwhelmingly joyous and lively. I sat there as it radiated up through my body. Tingling and waves of sensation running over my entire body. Playful energy as if it were reflecting a state of euphoria. I picked up the phone and called her, knowing she was home.

"Hi bud!" she answered as if she knew it was me.

"What on earth are you doing?" I inquired.

"I'm refinishing this fireplace mantel downstairs and I was listening to music and thinking of you! I was thinking how great it was to have found this new friend of mine and how happy I was about it. You are a ray of sunshine for me. You were a gift for my birthday. I know my sister Karen the Angel brought us together."

"Well I sure could feel it bud. I was sitting on this couch and all of a sudden the door opened on the energy and it came flooding over me. That's why I had to call."

Beth's honey voice came back through the phone.

"Neat! I don't know how this is all working but I could feel you when you feel the energy. It's kind of like getting a response from what I sent you, like I could tell you felt it. I know what you mean it kind of goes all through your body and fills you with some sort of energy, for lack of a better word."

"That's it Beth. Strange eh?"

We talked about the day and some other minor things before we said "see ya later" and hung up. It wasn't more than a few minutes later and I had such a rush of this energy that I couldn't stand it. It was overwhelming and it pushed me into the seat. It was enormously pleasurable but quite disconcerting. I forced myself out of the seat and back to the phone. I punched Beth's number into the phone once again. The phone rang less than once and I heard her voice.

"Ha ha ha ha so?"

"What are you up to? Now what are you doing? You nearly knocked me off the seat here and I don't know if I can take much more!" I whispered into the phone quietly.

"Ha ha ha ha ha! I love it! This is so cool!" Beth's voice showed a wide smile on her face as she spoke.

"I decided to take it a bit further so I cranked up some music and sprayed some perfume in the air and made believe you were here dancing with me. When I felt it connect with you I pushed more back and I got more back. It was incredible! Ha ha ha !"

"Oh boy. This is too much Beth. I can't take much more so take it easy for a while okay?"

"Okay."

"Now go finish your mantel and take it easy for a bit so I can regroup."

"Okay. Love ya, see ya."

"Same here, see ya!" I said as I hung up the phone.

I looked at Sadie as she gave me a strange look but said nothing. That calm pond image matched her composure.

Life was quite odd from day to day with this connection and this "energy." Not only could I feel it as I walked the plant floor but then there were the connections where I would know what was up with Beth at the same time. When she was depressed I would even get a feeling of her head on my shoulder and a whiff of her perfume about me when there was no one there. No source for perfume or the smell I had. But I smelled it. I could feel the pressure of her head against my shoulder as if it were real as well, even though I never physically experienced her head on my shoulder.

I knew Beth was feeling me at the same time when she connected like that. One time I was having a hell of a week and this particular day everything was coming to a head. I had four major problems in the plant that just weren't getting resolved. I had a number of people working on them diligently, their efforts bore no fruit and the problems remained.

Every spare moment I spent involved in one or the other to try to push things along. It seemed to me these problems were like any other that I dealt with. If you tried hard enough, and put in enough effort, you would resolve them. It seemed to be working opposite that, as the more effort I expelled, the worse it got. Why couldn't I control this situation? Why wasn't it working? I thought I must not be trying hard enough. I was picking up my safety glasses off my desk to go back out and attack these problems some more and then the phone rang. I picked it up.

"A.J. Aaron"

"Just step out of it! I don't know what the hell you are doing or what's going on but I can feel you and you are ready to pop! Just step out of whatever it is. Let it go!" Beth's voice cried to me from the receiver. I stood there in awe of her recognizing me to be having this bad a problem at this moment.

"What? What are you talking about?" I asked, as I couldn't believe what she was saying.

"Step out of it. You are a wreck and trying to control what should be let go. You're trying so hard to control it is not going to kill it. Just do me a favor and mentally let it go. Go have a coffee and a smoke if you want, but tell yourself you're letting it go and do so. Mentally, let the problems go and see what happens, okay?" I can feel the way you are right now and it's not good. Do it, okay?"

I thought about what she said, and then I bought a cup of coffee from the machine and went outside. I lit a cigarette and tried to visualize stepping away from these four problems as Beth had asked. It certainly couldn't hurt since I was getting nowhere as things were. I gave the problems away in my mind and released them. I finished the coffee in a relaxed state and enjoyed my smoke and went back inside the plant feeling relaxed and relieved as if they were fixed already.

I made my way past the problems. The first was gone and things were running. The engineer working on the problem was smiling and laughing with those he was working on it with. I had to ask.

"So what's up?"

"All set! It's running great now. I'm not quite sure what was the last variable that did it but it seems to have all come together, finally." He beamed with pride that it was resolved.

"Nice job guys! I owe ya all a beer. Thanks for all the hard work." I moved on to the next problem, and the next, and the next. All the rest were gone too. In fifteen minutes I was back in my office and went to the phone. I called Beth.

"So?" She answered the phone.

"Thanks Angel! You are my Angel! Everything is all squared away so I'm getting the hell out of here before something else blows up. Your advice worked!"

"Glad to hear it. I knew it would. You feel better now I can tell. I'll let ya go.
Love ya, see ya."

"You too Angel. Later."

I packed up my briefcase, threw the business paper onto an engineer's desk and walked out the door to go home. It amazed me at how well that simple action of releasing control solved those problems, or at least it seemed to. Was it a coincidence? Maybe. I hadn't spoken to Beth for a few days, yet she managed to call at the very apogee when I was in chaos. It all resolved itself. All things should be so easy.

I went to work the next day and told Brad about what had happened. He looked at me, not the least bit surprised.

"See how easy it can be?"

"What about this energy stuff. Can I use it for anything else?" I asked him as the beat of the plant pounded and hummed around us.

"Sure you can. Try to use it to resolve people issues when they arise. Release control, push that energy into the meeting and watch what happens. Minimize your input and just push the energy into the others and release control, letting it go the way it does and see what happens."

"You mean pull energy and force it into the meeting?"

"Yeah, just push that energy out there to the participants and watch the results."

"I have a meeting coming up today to resolve some issues between Toby and Darek. I'm not looking forward to it a bit, since I know what those two will be doing. They'll try to tear each other down in front of me and then try to have me make a call on who is right and wrong. Then, one of them will have won and one will have lost. Then I'll have only one of the two motivated to do anything while the other figures out a way to get back at the winner."

"Sounds like a perfect opportunity to me!?" Brad grinned as he snickered knowing what the meeting would be like.

"Okay I'll do it!" I said as we parted.

I took the Darek and Toby meeting into the foremen's lounge area because it's a more private place than my office where everyone could walk by and get the drift of what was going on. The lounge was closed off and only supervisors went in there. I had them both sit down as did I.

"Okay guys. You both know the issue we need to resolve here and there seems to be some disagreement as to what should happen, or what has been happening. Why don't you guys go over the issue from each of your view points, and see if we can resolve the disparity."

I sat back in my chair and looked at each of them as I drew energy up through my hands and feet, and as it flowed into me, I pushed it out to the two of them with a favorable intent. I checked their auras as they started talking and could see them go from red to yellow. I listened to the conversation as it turned into the most professional and positive a discussion I had ever heard these two have. The meeting lasted all of maybe ten minutes. Before I knew what had occurred, the two of them were shaking hands and getting up in full agreement. I had no input. There was no nudging or directing by me. No taking of sides or making a winner or looser. I had to acknowledge this to them.

"Toby, Darek, I have to say something here. I always knew you two were a couple of the best supervisors on this planet but I never quite saw it demonstrated so well. The way you two just worked together on an issue, that was touchy for each of you, makes me proud as hell to be associated with you both. I was fully expecting a bit of a battle here, but you made me proud instead. I can't tell you how much this means to me. You have both reached a new level of expertise in dealing with these problems. Congratulations and keep up the good work."

I shook both of their hands as they beamed in my praise for them. They left the room as partners rather than adversaries. It worked! The energy does seem to have a power to it. How can it though? What was it? Could it just be coincidence? I wasn't entirely sure what just transpired but it was a good thing for sure. I guess maybe I had learned something here.

So where was I these days. Let's see. Feeling energy through my hands and feet and from people, seeing auras, being connected to another person who was recently a total stranger but that I felt more intimate with than anyone I ever knew. What was this energy? How does releasing control bring about solutions to problems? How does leaving an interaction on its own, with nothing other than this energy to feed it, somehow make the interaction go smoothly instead of a confrontation? None of this made any sense to me, but it was real, as far as I could tell. Or, this whole darn thing was an elaborate dream I would soon wake up from. Or, I was imagining all of this while I was awake, and God knows what I was really doing while I imagined all of this.

I went home that day feeling a new (and better?) world was opening before me. I ate dinner and relaxed, and picked up a book off the shelf to read.

Happenings

Over the next month things kept happening that were, well, unexplainable. Things that drives a logic driven person like me crazy or, is it the fact that I'm crazy that I **think** these things are happening. Hmmm, in order to give you a flavor for some of these things without telling you all the details of events leading up to and surrounding them, I will simply state them. Those that follow came out of my notes from that time.

10/17/97 - I mentally asked Beth to call me and she didn't. I could tell she wasn't home. As I felt for her I could feel a playful energy about me in surges that rolled from place to place. I knew she was out and she must be dancing and having a good time. I thought about her having too much to drink and sent out a caution to her since her energy felt a bit tipsy.

10/18/97 - I received two pieces of mail from Beth. One was for the Aaron Family, and one was for Sadie. They were cards. When I held them I thought to call her and then figured I'd wait until later. Then I couldn't stop myself and had to call then. She answered the phone with, "What took you so long? I've been asking you to call for a few minutes already." I asked her if she had a good time last night and she said she did. She said her and her boyfriend Doug had fun dancing. She said she felt me call to her last night and so she sent me energy over and over. She said she had something tell her to not have another drink and to be careful going home.

10/20/97 - It's Monday and I was tired all day yesterday and still was tired today. Feel lethargic and feel something is wrong regarding Beth. I call and Beth answers the phone and says, "You want to know what's wrong right?" "Of course" I say. She says she chipped a hunk of a front tooth off and was pretty upset about it and felt drained all day Sunday and still was beat. (Fatigue is also a part of MS). Am I picking up on her physical feelings this well?

One particularly relevant thing happened on October 8, 1997. I was at work and had had enough of it before lunch time had even arrived. It was a beautiful day out and the sun called to me. Well, I thought I could take a half day vacation but what would I do? Then I thought about Lady of Lourdes what a good place it would be to unwind and relax a bit in the sun. I called Sadie and let her know I was going, grabbed a burger for lunch and headed for the shrine.

I reached the parking lot and could feel the energy there though not as much as the first time. I felt it as it flowed up into my hands and feet and filled my body. The warmth of the sun felt good on this fall day as the chipmunks chattered and squeaked all around, running through leaves in the woods. I went into the gift shop and purchased two white candles for lighting in the candle house. They were supposed to be able to burn for seven days.

I went to the candle house to light a candle for Beth and another for my friend Vinny who had a terrible accident and was now paralyzed. The smell of the paraffin filled the area under the roof where the temperature was about thirty degrees warmer than outside. There must have been over a hundred of these tall candles lit there, over a hundred wishes and prayers to help people. These were wishes for the sick and those in pain, wishes for the distraught.

I lit the candles and said a prayer for both and put some money in the offering can. I then turned and noticed no one else was there but me right now. I left the candle house and walked over to the stream of water running over the stone from the original shrine in Lourdes in France. I took a paper cup from the dispenser and drank some of the water running over the stone. Then, I sat in the sun and I meditated.

I felt someone's presence next to me, I opened my eyes and turned to look. On the aisle was a little old lady with red hair smiling at me. She was hunched over and limped closer to me with some effort. She had a prayer card with a picture of the lady in the grotto on it and she was pushing it toward me as she said,

"Here son, meditate on this. It will help."

I took it from her and thanked her as her shining, loving eyes met mine.

I scanned it quickly, and when I was done I looked up to see where she was but she wasn't in sight. I don't know where that tiny old woman could have gone to so fast but she was no where in sight. The card said the following:

<u>Prayer to Our Lady of Lourdes</u>

O ever immaculate virgin, Mother of mercy, healer of the sick, refuge of sinners, comfort of the afflicted, you know my wants, my troubles, my sufferings, deign to cast upon me a look of mercy. By appearing in the Grotto of Lourdes, you were pleased to make it a privileged sanctuary, whence you dispense your favors, and already many sufferers have obtained the cure of their infirmities, both spiritual and corporal. I come therefore, with unbounded confidence to implore your maternal intercession. Obtain, O loving Mother, the grant of my request. I will endeavor to imitate your virtues, that I may one day share your glory, and bless you in eternity.

Amen.

50 days' indulgence

Joseph Schrembs

Archbishop-Bishop of Cleveland

I put a date on it and put it in my planner booklet in my back pocket. I sat there a bit longer and noticed the chipmunks were now very quiet. After a bit, I thought I'd walk about and see if I could find them. There were so many making such a racket when I arrived they must be around here somewhere.

I went to the path through the woods where the Stations of the Cross were placed. There were statues of Angels and Saints there as well. I stopped and read a stone that had words carved in it. It said, "If it be God's will, not thy will, then it shall be." Hmm I guess that was my answer to all my questions?" I made a note of the statement and moved on. I walked up the hill and out of the Stations of the Cross path and onto a road that wound around the shrine. I completed the circle and went back to the car. I drove home and relaxed on the deck and read for a bit before supper.

The next day I spoke to Beth on the phone and she told me about a dream she had last night. She said it was a beautiful place but she couldn't recognize it. She described it with labored speech. She spoke with pauses, I could tell her MS wasn't good today.

"There were flowers against a stone wall,... and a statue there. It looked like it could be a holy shrine or something. I walked around the place and there was a cave in the woods with angels in front. There was a little old lady there, that I saw, several times. I could see her, from behind, but not from the front. She was a tiny thing with red hair. It was a beautiful, peaceful, place. I wish I could go there again."

I was shocked as I stammered.

"I uh, I was there yesterday. I said a prayer for you and Vinny. Vinny was the supervisor I worked with that had the horrible accident. I took a half day vacation and went there to relax."

"What place was that? Where did you go?"

"It was Lady of Lourdes. It's a shrine out this way. It is a model of the one in France."

"Why did you go there? How did you find out about it?"

I told Beth the story when Tom and I were delivering the wines and ended up there. I told her how I felt the energy there back in August before we met and how that came about. I told her about the little red headed lady and the card.

"Read the card to me okay?"

"Sure" I read her the card.

"50 days indulgence. What does that mean?"

"I don't know. I guess you need to give it fifty days."

"When did you go, yesterday? Hang on."

"That's Thanksgiving day! Oh my God! You were talking about me coming out for that week to meet the family and get away from here so I could break this memory of people dying on Thanksgiving. That's incredible!"

"Well maybe you will be here."

"I can't go out there. Your wife is great but I don't think she'll quite understand this plus, I don't have the money to fly out there. And I'm not gonna drive that far with the shape I'm in. I'd probably fall asleep on the way. Not to mention my car isn't in the greatest shape lately."

"I don't know bud. I have a pretty strong feeling that you'll be here. That you have to be here then. I'm not sure how but I think it's gonna happen."

We chatted a bit and I got off the phone. I hadn't told Sadie much about the trip to Lourdes when I got home yesterday but now I thought I better. I told her about the card, the stone with the "will" words, then talking to Beth and what she dreamt. When I was through her expression remained unchanged and still calm as a pond. Then she spoke.

"I'm buying her tickets to fly out for that week. I'll call Yelka tomorrow and set it up for her to come in on the Saturday before Thanksgiving and return the Sunday after Thanksgiving. This is something that needs to be done. You need to take her to the shrine on Thanksgiving day."

I was thrilled to have my wife come up with this suggestion. I called Beth and checked the days with her. She couldn't believe it of course, yet at the same time, she could. All of this was so unbelievable anyway.

Sadie made arrangements the next day. She even got a really good deal. Much better than I'd gotten to travel there for work.

Well, I guess this ball was rolling, but to where I wasn't sure. Thank God my wife understood this or at least wasn't letting it get to her. I sure didn't want to mess my marriage up over all of this. But I had to follow this through, so it was a good thing Sadie was as she was, the calm pond, or I don't know what would have happened. A lot of people would be too insecure to let a person of the opposite sex come into their home to visit their spouse for a week. Regardless of the circumstances! I doubt most men would risk it if they were in my position. But how could I avoid it? We both faced our fears and continued with this craziness, trusting that what was happening, was for a reason.

Throughout the month of October and November before Beth's arrival, there were what became standard signals I'd notice from time to time. It was that open connection to each other. No need to meditate to connect either, an open connection. When she was depressed I would smell the perfume and feel her head on my shoulder. When she was happy, I could tell from the feel of the energy. When she was tired I could feel it. It was to the point where it was so regular it was almost an intrusion at times.

I continued to meditate on and off and usually connected not only with Beth's already open connection but deeper with wherever Beth was at the time. I would get fleeting glimpses of what she was doing or of her surroundings. I could do it as easily as closing my eyes and I'd snap myself into that other realm. Then I'd say, "Take me to Beth" and I'd be there. I would then be able to understand and verify the things I saw when we spoke at a later time.

One time I was on the phone with Beth and I closed my eyes while she spoke and sent myself there mentally. The colors and textures I described to her from my fleeting glimpses were her surroundings. Later, when I actually had a business trip out that way for a week, she invited me and another work mate to her house. The same house she was in while I spoke to her on the phone many times. The same house I had fleeting flashes of colors and textures that I saw in my mind. When I walked into the house, the sight gave me a complete deja' vu. I sat down in the recliner. The things I saw from that seat I had already seen and actually knew the texture and feel of them. It was astounding to me how accurately I had developed the picture of this place before I had ever been there. I never saw a picture and the only time Beth described it to me was when I saw something and she explained to me what it was.

Was I creating this picture from her describing things to me, or had I actually seen them? Well, the fact that I was telling her what I saw and that she was confirming to me what it was, meant that at least in part it was from my input and not hers. If in fact it was from my input how did it happen? Was I astral projecting? Was I remote viewing? Why didn't I see her when I went to where she was?

When she was in the hospital for a time with a scare about her heart I described a person standing by the window in her room as they looked out. I described them from the flashes of pictures in my mind. I could even tell something about the person's emotions at the time and what they were like. I described this on the phone to Beth and what I described was the nurse that was in her room at that very moment looking out the window. I got her hair color and length, the view from the window, the place she was standing, what kind of person she was and how she was feeling.

How was this happening? I still wasn't sure. Was she lying to me and just agreeing and reinforcing what I was saying? I had a hard time believing that since I knew lying was a difficult, if not impossible thing for her. But what if someone were an expert at lying? Wouldn't they then be able to say they could never lie and be able to give that impression? Again, hard for me to believe about Beth though possible.

Another time I was on my deck and hadn't meditated or connected to Beth in a long time. It was after the time when we were having the open connection and I wanted to see if it was still possible. I sat down and got myself comfortable. It was about

seventy five degrees with a nice breeze blowing. I had music playing
out on the deck that was relaxing. I sat in the chair facing east while
the shade from the tall maples and the breeze kept me cool. I sipped
a bit of the fresh lemonade and put the glass on the table.

I let all my muscles relax and my head rest against the back
of the chair. I closed my eyes and took three deep, slow, breaths
filling my lungs all the way and letting it out all the way. I visualized
all the colors of the rainbow and imagined the corresponding
sensations of them in their chakra location on my body. (I had read
about this technique somewhere and started using it as it seemed to
help to focus me.) I could feel my thighs relax and shrink away from
the fabric of my jeans. I could feel an itch on my face and let it pass.

My breathing was diminishing as my heart rate slowed. (My
at rest heart rate is sixty four beats per minute but meditating drops it
to fifty four.) I could hardly feel myself breathe as I started to ask
myself what I wanted out of this session. I asked mentally to go to
Beth. I stopped all thought and any thoughts arriving were released
and not responded to. I felt the shift. In a matter of moments I saw
something very vividly. There was white around me, and it felt like I
was in a corridor or something. Then, all of a sudden, there was a
woman before me with thick long black hair and a black knit top.
She was staring right into my eyes with a look of terror, or fright,
and screamed at me as she held up her arms. It scared me so much I
almost came right out of the meditation but I didn't want to stop. Did
she actually see me? Who the heck was she? Was I in some strange
form floating around this woman's house? That view left me, then, as

I relaxed again and opened up, all I saw was a woman's thin ankle with black sheer stockings, and flat dark loafers with the toe pointed to the floor and a hand on the ankle scratching it. Then it left me.

I came out of the meditation and noted the time. I had been in meditation for about an hour. It was three thirty when I came out of it. I went about the rest of the day. I knew she would be out and so I figured I'd call later when I knew she would be home.

At about six in the evening I called her.

"Hi bud!"

"Hi, I just got in. How's things going?"

"Good good. What were you up to today?"

"I went to a birthday party at a friend's apartment. It was a nice way to spend the afternoon."

"Oh yeah, tell me about it. Anything interesting happen?"

"Not really, though I did scare the heck out of her. She wanted to change her top cause it was warm so she went to the bedroom. I forgot she had gone down there and wasn't thinking about it when I went to go down the corridor to the bathroom. When I flew around the corner I almost plowed her down and she screamed. We both laughed after but you should have seen her. She looked like she saw a ghost. I felt bad I scared her so much."

"Describe her to me. What does she look like?"

"Well she's not as tall as me and she has really black, really thick long hair. The top she changed into was a black sleeveless knit top. When I plowed into her I was in her hallway and the walls were the standard white."

"Beth, I think I know how I'm seeing this stuff now. I saw exactly what you described. When did that happen do you remember?"

"I think it must have been around three sometime. What do you mean you know how you see this stuff?"

"Well, I always thought I was seeing things by just having my consciousness there somehow. But now, after seeing her face and having it feel like she saw me I know where I was. If I think back to the other times I did this too, I never saw you from outside. I never saw you from behind or in front. So that means what I saw was through your eyes. I literally perceived what you perceived."

"That makes sense. Wow that means you were inside me. In my body." I could hear her smile at the thought.

"Yup... I guess. HA ha ha kinda strange huh? I wonder if you'd let me in when other things were happening that were more personal. Ha ha ha!"

"Ha ha ha I don't think so bud!"

"Okay now I had one more thing I saw and that's it. There was a foot with flat shoes on and black sheer stockings. The view I had was as if the legs were crossed and there was someone scratching their ankle. It happened after the fright scene."
"I wore dark green, almost black, leather loafers with black sheer knee highs today. You must have seen me scratching my ankle when I sat down. I think I have a bug bite there but I couldn't see one. It itched like hell."

"Well that's that! Now the question is, why is this happening and why is it only with you and what good is it?" I could hear Beth's smirk on the phone and almost see her shake her head as she responded to my comment.

"There you go again. Why do you always need to ask why? Who cares why or how? It's neat. You're not a lunatic!! It happens. We share something. So let it be."

"But there has to be a better reason for why we were brought together this way and why we can do these things?"

"Why does there have to be a better reason? Answer that instead."

"Okay okay."

We talked a bit more about the week's happenings and then finished our conversation.

"Okay bud, I'll talk to you later. Enjoy the rest of the daylight."

Her melodic voice then came back through the receiver.

"You too and say hi to Sadie and the kids. Love ya, see ya"

"You too.... see ya."

The time for Beth's visit rapidly approached. Before I knew it I was at the airport gate waiting for her plane to show up. I hadn't seen her since September and it was now November. I was a bit nervous about how I'd feel when I did see her. I wasn't certain this stranger wasn't going to make a mess of my life when she stayed with us for the week, but that was my warped logic speaking from fear, and not what I intuitively knew about her and us. The plane pulled up to the gate.

I stood up and moved over to where they would enter the terminal, standing back to not block the traffic coming off the jet. I completely missed her getting off, though I watched as each person went their way. She came around me from behind and gave me a hug, startling me. I guess I looked confused the way she looked back at me. Her hair is that of an older woman, and she had the appearance of someone maybe 60 or so. She spoke before me as I was still in a daze.

"Hey bud! Ugh! Love to feel you near again! Ugh!"

Beth gives me a squeeze as I hug her back unemotionally.

"What's the matter bud? You didn't even see me getting off the plane."

"I uh, I didn't recognize you."

Beth steps back and gives me a good look.

"That's okay bud. It's sooooo good to see you." She said as she moved closer again and gave me a hug. That felt familiar at least.

"Ah okay. Yea Sorry. Just been a tough time for me lately. C'mon let's get your bags, and we can go home."

Beth takes my arm as she slightly drags her one leg and somewhat struggles to walk smoothly. Her tall, graceful frame still managing to have grace, even with the slight MS imperfection, moves off with me toward baggage claim. I can't help but think I am absolutely insane at this point. It's her no doubt, but it's not! Can my memory of her be this bad? Has she changed so much in so little time since I last saw her?

It was a cloudy, gloomy, day still. We get into the car and Beth looks younger again. Much more like 40 than 60. She seems to have transformed before my eyes. I now remember her well, though I was still trying to figure out what happened.

"Boy I don't know how I didn't recognize you! My Angel buddy!"

Beth leaned over toward me and grabbed my hand and squeezed it.

"God it feels so good to be with you! Seems like we've known each other forever and been apart that long too."

"I know. It seems strange. I know all about you and yet I know nothing since you haven't told me very much, and we were only together for a few hours. But I don't even need to know anything. I just feel so good around you."

"You didn't look like you felt too well at the airport."

"I really didn't recognize you. But now I do, and it seems you look different now. Very different."

"I look younger now huh?"

"Yes! How did you know? Never mind that question. Ha ha ha."

"No I didn't read your mind, I don't think, or did I, but since you told me, anyway, I thought **I** was nuts, but I guess we both are. See, I sometimes see an old man in you. The face and hair and body and all. Glad you saw a different me too. Now I know it's not just me."

"So what do you look like!?"

"What do you think? I'm not an OLD lady."

"Yea yea okay. This is gonna be a tough week I think. I think we're gonna learn some more things, or at least test our sanity further."

Beth slips over and reaches to kiss me on the cheek and then slides back into her seat. Holding my right hand and rubbing it.

"I can't wait. Whatever it is, I'm ready for it! I have my bud with me!"

She had again become the woman I knew before, and the familiarity returned. It was as if she was someone else when she got off that plane. I couldn't explain it, didn't know what had happened, and for the time I just disregarded it, and began to enjoy having my psychically intimate friend beside me.

The weather was typical for a Thanksgiving week in Cleveland, overcast skies and cool air. We picked up the kids at a friends' house where my wife had arranged for them to be while she was at work so I could go get Beth. They took to Beth quite naturally and we went to our house. Beth got her things squared away and we cooked dinner.

I seemed to know her likes and dislikes in food and beverages as if we had always known each other. That week was like a reunion with a family member and not some strange woman I had met in another state. Sadie and Beth got along well and there was no sense of jealousy or animosity. Every night after the kids went to bed we would put on some music and the three of us would chat downstairs with a fire burning in the woodstove.

One night, after Sadie had gone to bed, Beth was sitting on the floor by the fire and I was on the couch as we were finishing up the evening. The music playing was an ethereal melody that seemed to vibrate directly inside of me. I looked at Beth and knew that she could feel it as well. We were connected as we were over the miles but we were just a matter of feet apart right now. As I looked at her I could see that she was feeling it.

"Yes, I feel it too," Beth said.

"Show me as it circulates up and down your body," I said.

She motioned with her hand as it moved over her and it didn't coincide to the music but it did coincide to the rhythm I was experiencing. We were literally connected in some manner to the vibration occurring in us and we were both experiencing the same blissful feeling it imparted.

"This is awesome, blissful, kinda like a full body orgasm. It almost feels like we shouldn't be doing it but we aren't doing anything." Beth said as she grinned at the pleasantness of the sensation.

It certainly was pleasant. It was similar to the connection over the miles but being there, but being able to see the other person as they reacted to it added another degree of enhanced satisfaction. Why did it happen? Was it the music? Was it just our being in proximity to each other and being open and relaxed? It faded after a bit and I closed up the stove for the night, shut off the lights and music and went to bed.

A New Reality

We did a number of things that week but nothing really dramatic, for the most part. We went shopping for baseball shirts and hats for Christmas for Beth to take back as Christmas presents. We ransacked gift shops and book stores. Went running for groceries and dropped the car off to be fixed. We visited some sights in Cleveland, and launched rockets with the kids and even picked up a Christmas tree and decorated it. Beth worked on a puzzle with Sadie and the kids as I watched a movie on television. It wasn't as if we had a visitor, it was as if someone had come home to us.

One evening after dinner, Beth and I went downstairs to have a smoke and her cup of tea and me my coffee. Sadie was taking a shower or something, and I don't remember where the kids were at the time, maybe outside. We were talking about our connection to each other and decided to test it a bit. In my hand I was playing with a colored disk left out from a game the kids had out.

"You know, I still have trouble with the fact we can be so connected. Maybe it's just a series of coincidences that looks like a connection? Maybe we really aren't."

"Oh coommmmmeee oooonnnn bud. Don't start that again. Why do you always have to question these things?"

"That's how I work! That's what makes me me! I have to!"

"But your driving yourself crazy!"

"I think I am crazy, and just not seeing it. I'm being delusional, and making excuses for it. Here let's try something."

"Beth, why don't you go sit at the bar facing out the window and I'll sit on the couch facing your back. We'll each have a set of these colored circles."

I showed her the one I held.

"I'll try to mentally let you know the one I'm holding, then you hold the one up that matches it so I can see it. Let's see how well we can do this on a formal basis. If all the connections we've have been having are real then we should be able to do this pretty easily."

I got up and went to a closet and took out some colored circular pieces from the kids toy box. The pieces are about two inches in diameter. I went back to Beth and helped her stand, took her to the bar at the end of the room and seated her. I sorted the disks out on the bar.

"What do you mean IF they are real. Why do you still not believe this is happening? I don't care, let's do it!" She huffed as she picked up a set of the seven different colored circles.

"You sit there with one set of seven, and I have a matching set. I'll go sit on the couch while you sit here facing away from me. If we beat the odds we're connected somehow. There is a one in seven chance of getting it right the first time. Then getting it right twice is one in 49, or 7 times seven. Then three times is 7 times 7 times 7 or uh, one in 343 and so on. Okay?"

Beth is laughing now as she gives me a peck on the cheek.

"You are nuts. You really are. Ha ha ha."

"C'mon!" I cried pleadingly.

"I'll do it I'll do it! Ha ha ha....Go!"

Beth motions for me to go to the couch. I sit and put the colors on my lap. I relaxed and felt our connection kick in, humming away.

"Okay, turn around and face the wall, leave your pieces on the bar until you decide which one I'm sending, then pick it up and let me see it."

Beth turns on the barstool laughing, and faces the wall. I pick a blue one and hold it in my hand as I close my eyes, and concentrate.

"Okay. Blue" Beth holds the matching blue one up and giggles like a little girl.

"One in seven chance. Lucky. Next one."

Beth remains turned facing away toward the windows behind the bar. The snow falls in the spotlights in back. I pick a yellow one and hold it closing my eyes again.

"Yellow!" Beth holds up the yellow circle between her fingers so I can see it. She still faces away. I open my hand, and show her.

"Uh look."

"Ha ha ha"

"One in 49. Still just luck."

"Not luck! Proof."

"Not yet. Again. Doubt it'll happen again."

I grab a green one, and before my eyes close, Beth raises hers and calls out.

"Green. 7 time 7 times 7 huh?"

"Yea 343. One in 343"

"Again!" She calls out. We do it quickly now. I just pick one out, and Beth calls. I grab an orange one.

Beth picks hers up and cries out waving it at me, "Orange! 7 times 7 times 7 times 7. 343 times 7 uh, let's see. 2100 plus 350 minus 49. Twenty four hundred and one to one odds of that happening!"

"Uh, yea."

"Again!"

"Uh"

"Again! We need to give you proof remember?"

"Okay, Okay!"

I go for the next one. I pick a Pur...

"Purple"

"Geez Beth! give me a chance to pick it up all the way okay? Purple!"

"Again!"

"Shit!"

I know she can't see a reflection in the window. The window is too high, there is a light outside and I'm sitting too low. The angles and the conditions are all wrong. I reach again but this time I pick up the same purple one.

"Purple again? Why did you pick the purple one again? Does that count?"

"YES! It does."

"Again!" Beth cries out.

"You're possessed, a witch or something!"

"I'm not a witch!"

I reach for another and grab a red one.

"Red!" She says less emphatically but very confidently without looking up as she counts on her fingers.

"7, times 7, times 7, times 7, times 7, times 7, times 7. 7 in a row. What's that come to?! A big coincidence?! Again!"

"Okay stop, enough!"

I get up, and go to a calculator on the bar. I punch in the numbers as I stand next to Beth. 7 times selecting the same one resulted in one chance in, eight hundred twenty three thousand, five hundred, and forty three, chances of that ever happening.

"Is that enough? Coincidence? Hmmm C'mon bud lets sit by the fire and just be together okay? No more tests. Just accept what's happening." She said as she slid off the barstool and came over to me as I stood and she gave me a hug.

I couldn't believe it. It was a couple of years later though that it struck me as to how unusual that result actually was. It seemed to come at a time when my belief in all of this stuff was starting to wane. The odds aren't as bad as the odds of winning the lottery but they are pretty bad. I wouldn't want to bet my life on those odds. I think I could honestly say that what was happening was real. We probably couldn't do it again if we tried, but it was something to help reinforce what was going on at the time.

The only other "strange" thing to happen that week was at Lady of Lourdes. It was Thanksgiving Day and the fifty days from when I had read that little old lady's card there. We all had a great Thanksgiving Day, baked stuffed shrimp feast for lunch and then Beth and I headed out to the shrine. I tried to get her to wear her winter coat as it was thirty degrees out but she insisted that her thin leather blazer would be fine.

It was a gorgeous sunny day but cold with a biting breeze. We walked to the candle house and I pulled the sheepskin collar of my bomber jacket up over my neck. Beth was smiling and not noticing the cold one bit. We lit some candles and said some silent prayers. Beth stood before the statue of Mary and a blue jay landed on the statue's head. As Beth looked up at the bird, it squawked loudly at Beth, tilted it's head and stared right into her eyes. Beth drank some of the water flowing from the grotto and we sat on one of the cold steel benches for a bit as we took in the view of the now silent retreat.

"You sure you're not cold?' I asked as I sat there with a chill.

"Are you kidding? Feel my hands and tell me I'm cold."

She took my hand between hers and she was very warm. It was as if a fire was lit inside of her thin bony frame..

"Now relax and be quiet for a bit," she said as she took her hands away and sat contentedly with a smile on her face.

As I looked at her in wonderment about why she wasn't cold she closed her eyes and appeared to be in a meditative bliss. The area became totally quiet. The birds stop their racket. The chipmunks stop there chirping. The squirrels running through the leaves were like the were never there. No sound. Utter silence. I looked around to confirm what was happening and then I looked at Beth.

It was at that point I could see a strange display of white flecks surrounding her. It was like fine snow in a street light as it swirled and enveloped her total form. Like snow except he flecks were a bluish white and shot here and there randomly. I couldn't follow one with my eyes as it disappeared and others appeared from nowhere. Now what kind of strange illusion was I encountering. Illusion? Reality? I didn't know.

I held my comments for a few minutes just watching the flecks to allow Beth her space till I saw she was ready. The light show subsided and then she turned and looked at me. I told Beth what I saw and she just shrugged it off.

"Beth, what do you think that was?"

"Oh c'mon. Here we go again. Analysis time…Who cares?"

"Did you feel anything?"

"I felt relaxed, warm, loved and your energy but really strong this time that's all."

"I don't think you felt my energy. I don't know. I wasn't feeling any energy since I was too caught up by what was happening."

"Not yours?"

"I don't know. I know the world doesn't go silent when I connect with you. This time it did. No birds or animals moving or anything." I told her about the flecks.

Let's go walk around a bit. Don't try to analyze anything okay?"

"K, You're not cold?"

"Not cold! Now c'mon!"

Beth grabbed my hand and pulled me from the bench and we went exploring the paths in the woods. When we went back to the car, I was relieved it warmed up quickly to drive the chill away from me, though Beth had no need yet for the heat the car gave us. We went home and told Sadie the story and relaxed doing a puzzle on a table by the fire.

The rest of the week was as thoroughly enjoyable as the first part. Even though we mostly just hung out together and didn't do anything spectacular, it was the most pleasant experience I've had in a number of years. I couldn't remember having a more relaxing vacation where I didn't once think, or speak of, work at all. It was like going to a home I hadn't been to forever, plus something. I think the something was the regained familiarity with this person who definitely wasn't a total stranger. The feeling was more like a close family member, closer than I ever experienced before. Could we have been in other lives with each other before? Could we be the things some called soul mates? If such things existed, I imagine this is what it would feel like. I wished I knew if there were such an explanation.

Then the day came that I had to take Beth back to the airport. It was time for her to go home. I never would have thought it would be so painful.

A New Reality

We made it to the airport with plenty of time. This day the sky was overcast and the air felt damp and foreboding. We did somehow manage to get front row parking, which helped to reduce the time and distance it took to drag Beth's stuff to check it in.

"Maybe it's the parking Angels we got in Chagrin Falls!" Beth noted.

"Ha ha yeah, maybe. I never did find a parking this good here before. Ha ha ha."

We checked in the bags, bought a drink and had a passerby take a picture of us with Beth's ever present camera. We said our good-byes, hugged and she got on the plane. I couldn't tell if it was me or her that I was feeling, but it was painful. I usually didn't get too emotional about people coming or going. Sadie and I live far from our original homes where we were raised so we were used to coming and going and saying goodbye. This time though it was affecting me, or was it Beth I was feeling. I really couldn't tell.

Watching Beth board the plane caused a pain in my heart area and a lump jammed up in my throat. I could feel the closeness of my tears but I fought them off. I sat in the window looking at the plane until it pulled from the gate. I knew we'd see each other again and felt we would always be in touch so why was this so painful? I never get this emotional about anything. I dealt with it as the plane left and I walked back through the throngs of people in the airport to the car.

The pain wasn't subsiding a bit. I walked to the car and the dreariness of the day matched my emotions; gray, sad and forlorn. I lit a cigarette but had trouble inhaling it without a shudder. I started the car and backed it out of the space. I was doing all I could to keep my emotions in check. As I started forward, another car backed out in front of me. I couldn't believe the license plate. It was three letters, and normally they would represent something else to me, but this time they tripped me over the edge and I had to comply with what it told me. The three letters for "son of a bitch" were on the plate, (SOB). No numbers or any other letters. This time I read the word, not the letters, I pulled in that parking space and sobbed. I wiped my eyes and shuddered until I composed myself for the ride home.

I managed to get under control and back somewhat to "normal", though that term was becoming something of a mystery at this point. I was fine until the next morning when I woke to myself being back in the same state as when I saw that license plate. I made a cup of coffee and went outside until I could compose myself for the day. It astounded me that I was reacting this way out of no intention of my own. I never got this way. Not since I was a little kid did I feel like this. Not even then that I could remember. All I could think was this person must be very important to me as I thought the first night I met her. She seemed to be almost literally, a physical part of me, or so it seemed. It felt like a piece of me left with her. I told myself this would end and I would be back to normal soon. After a couple of hours I was better again.

It didn't take long for things to get worse at Beth's end. When she was out things were great even though she had all that medication to take for all her MS related maladies. When she got home to her life there things deteriorated. There were problems at home for her and her relationship with her boyfriend was in trouble. The next thing I knew I was calling to see what was wrong and her roommate Jan was telling me how she went into the emergency room last night. Beth had problems with chest pains and trouble breathing, etc. "Well, so much for Lady of Lourdes miracles," I started to think. What was that sparkle stuff all around her if it didn't heal her? More of my imagination acting up I guess.

I wanted to run out there and make sure she was taken care of but there was no way to do that. The feeling I got about this was not indicating there was anything wrong with her either. I **knew** she would be fine. I talked to her a couple of times a day (at lunch and then after supper), until they were done poking and prodding her, and she went home nine days after she went in. There was a purpose to all of it, or so it seemed. She was definitely experiencing a lack of love at home at the time and that could have been causing all the pains in her heart since the nine day hospital stay revealed no medical problems. This situation though seemed to help resolve some of those issues by waking up those around her.

Unfortunately things still got worse. She was home and had gotten a clean bill of health from the doctor. But don't forget, she still has MS and all the associated problems with depression and fatigue. And the issues that were there with her loved ones hadn't gone away entirely. When I spoke with her she seemed to be getting worse in terms of depression and anxiety and her speech was getting worse. The speech and depression are related to MS and I could tell by her pauses and stalls when she spoke that she wasn't getting better, but worse.

When she went to her Neurologist for an MS checkup, he took one look at her and had a fit. He couldn't believe she let herself go so long without calling him. She had lost weight since the last visit and he could tell her depression was severe just by looking at her. She was only 114# at five foot ten inches tall and he had known her since she had been diagnosed with MS over twenty years ago. He prescribed something for the depression now. I know she was taking six pills when she visited and this would make seven in addition to the intramuscular injections she had to give herself every three days that left welts on her skin.

I wished I could help her but I didn't know how. All I could do was be there on the phone for her. Then one day, I couldn't tell exactly when it started, Beth seemed to be better. Her speech was smoother and faster in her responses. Her depression was going away. She stopped taking the depression medication again and she was still okay. It seemed there might be a light at the end of the tunnel.

I personally was having a hard time with all of this. It was difficult to believe I wasn't in fact going insane and these experiences were real. I ended up coming across some information though that helped to put these things in the realm of some possibility at least. Some of it came at this point to offer some relief and some of it later. I'll include a basic part that helped me realize that what was happening may be possible in some still unknown way. Science to the rescue.

Science To The Rescue

I'd heard about the concept of us being not so material and solid as we like to think we are. Having had an engineering education I was exposed to a lot of information that was available on this but never really thought about it too much. We just learned about decay rates and nuclear reactor design and chemical interactions, but not about the space in an atom and what that might mean. Heck, that was too off base for an engineer to think about. In the midst of these strange happenings, I saw something on television, and then went searching for some more detail on it. I went through my nuclear engineering books and chemistry books but ended up finding it on the web. I found a quick, concise statement about the nature of nuclear structure (nuclear not nuke-yuler as so many people like to pronounce it.)

The web site was a government web site. It was produced by the Nuclear Science Division - Lawrence Berkley National Laboratory. (http://www.lbl.gov/abc/Basic.html.). The section was on nuclear structure.

As most of us are now aware, our bodies and everything in this world are made up of molecules that are made up of atoms. The atoms connect together to form the molecules. The atoms are made of a nucleus that contains photons and neutrons and electrons revolve around the nucleus, in orbits. Thus, an atom has an interior center made of a couple of things and then the orbiting electrons that are like little satellites. The neat part is all the space between the electrons and the nucleus. This isn't anywhere close to scale since it wouldn't fit on the page if it were.

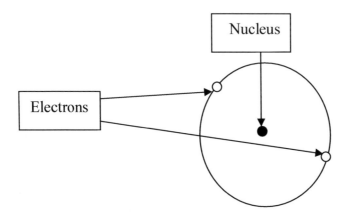

There are many arrangements of different orbits around a nucleus at varying distances and numbers of electrons. That is what makes up the different elements. The thing that is neat is the scale. The Nucleus is 1/10,000th the size of the atom (the diameter taken at the outer ring where the electrons orbit.) That means, if the nucleus were one inch in diameter, the electron would have to be 5000 inches or 416.7 feet away. It doesn't sound very solid does it. When atoms join together to form molecules they don't get their nuclei stuck together, heck no, they share orbits with the electrons. So what is matter? Mostly empty space. And everything is made from these.

"So what!" you say. Well, look at your hand and see the illusion of solidity that this creates for you to perceive. If we can perceive solidity from something so non-solid, why can't we also, somehow, perceive something non solid that isn't appearing to us visibly, or, from the senses. Ultraviolet light exists but we can't see it. Some falcons can but we can't.

"Well…" you say, "That thing in the center seems pretty solid so maybe that's what we feel and perceive." First off, remember again that molecules aren't joined together nucleus to nucleus but electron orbit to electron orbit. Additionally, to make that seemingly solid nucleus there are the protons and neutrons, but each of those consist of smaller particles yet that are called quarks, of which there are two varieties; Up quarks and down quarks. A proton consists of two up-quarks and a down-quark and a neutron consists of two down quarks and an up-quark. Add to this some more quarks that were discovered called, "charm", "strange", "bottom" and "top" (Note that scientists have a sense of humor as evidenced by those names) along with neutrinos and a muon and a heavier electron called a "tau" and two other particles similar to the neutrino called a "muon neutrino" and a "tau neutrino". Then, add to this, the fact that each of these particles has an anti-particle partner. Quite a soup but that is the key. A SOUP not a stew, not a cake but a soup. More like a broth with some particles in it and the particles have loosely scattered particles inside of them and inside of those particles more particles. So, mostly, the liquid of this soup is empty space. And this is what we *perceive* to be solid.

I came to find out later yet that the particles, in this soup, are made up of (it is currently believed by the physics community) strings that vibrate, and these strings, depending on their frequency of vibration, give the characteristic to the matter it makes up. Yes, you might say that it is a musical symphony that makes up matter. (See, "The Elegant Universe" (New York and London: W.W. Norton Co.1999) by Brian Greene, a Rhodes Scholar with a doctorate from Oxford University highly regarded for his work in Quantum physics.)

Now, if we really aren't solid, and neutrinos from the sun are blasting through our bodies all the time, and these strings vibrate, and the vibration defines the characteristics of the matter they make up, then why can't the vibrations actually resonate as strings would on a violin when one string is stroked and the other vibrates when a resonance is hit? Why can't one person's vibration affect another person's vibration along the similar receptors that are of the same note, or ability to resonate. Why can't this seemingly empty space receive these signals, per se, that arrive from a harmonious source? Or why can't one that doesn't resonate also feel the harsh non harmony that another vibration would create.

Can we prove it? It hasn't been yet. Not to most peoples satisfaction. Of course no one has ever physically proved there is a God, or Angels, either but most people believe in them. There is a possibility of it though, at least conceptually. We can't physically prove there are eleven dimensions either, though mathematically they are there. So what do you do? What do I do? I at least have a niche in my brain that says it is possible this can happen to me and that I am not going insane. Of course this will need further support along the way as all changes in thinking do. I received more evidence for myself in very short notice. It was as if to say, "Pay attention darn it and start to believe it!!" I guess I was feeling kind of like the quote I heard but never knew where it came from.

"He who believes needs no explanation. He who does not will have no explanation that is sufficient."

A good quote. I guess I was somewhere in between. What happened next helped to make me believe more fully though.

Another One!

Well, my friend in PA was getting a bit better but my own life seemed to keep me pretty much at wits end. My boss's boss was riding him, and he was riding me. I had been a Plant Manager for almost nine years now and had worked for my present boss for about fifteen years. I had never gotten anything but an "exceeds" review from him or any other boss I had. Now that he was under the gun, so was I, and a whipping post was in order. That was me.

To top it off there were a couple of legal cases at work that were typical examples of our litigious society and how people tried to get a buck from anything. In addition, a wonderful supervisor of mine (Vinny) had a bad accident at his son's bachelor party and now had brain damage. I had a plant that was overstuffed with parts it didn't need from feeder plants that had gone crazy to absorb all their overhead and from over ordering from suppliers, that my boss insisted on, to try to put out backlog. Grievance meetings that were no longer substantial since we had a new Chief Steward in the Union that didn't know what he was doing. ISO Audits in process to get us certified. The plant statement had incredibly inaccurate numbers that the accountants couldn't explain, numbers that said that 30% of what I made was variance from methods or machine variation. Impossible numbers. It felt as if the world had turned against me. I had it. I was ready for a change. The last thing I needed was to complicate my life by adding any unexplainable things to it! But, you know how that goes.

I went on a trip out of state to have a meeting and show some of our Mexican personnel around our plant up there. We had chartered the jet and seven of us that went to dinner that night then went out for a drink. It was "Fat Tuesday", the day before Lent. Lent is a Catholic event to prepare for Easter. Well, "Fat Tuesday" is the last day for pigging out before being good until Easter. In New Orleans they have Mardi Gras. Well this year, up north where we were, they thought they'd try that a bit too.

On February 24, 1998 at the state university's night life area, I got a chance for some relaxation with another of my supervisors, who was named Ed and who was also a good friend, while our Mexican friends enjoyed themselves. We were sitting at the bar chatting. Ed noticed a woman that didn't fit in with the rest of the crowd there that night. Since this was a college town there were appropriately aged people out on the town. This one was older and maybe in her mid thirties. She was normal looking except for the fact that she was smoking a cigar.

"A.J., look at that girl with the cigar! Kinda strange huh?"

"What? Ha ha yeah, I guess so."

We went back to our conversation about work and things and then the next thing I knew there was that woman ordering a beer beside me at the bar rail. I turned to see her and she smiled as she spoke.

"Hi how are you tonight?"

"I'm doing fine. Thanks for asking. Where did all these people come from all of a sudden?"

"There's a bar hop tonight and this is the last stop. There were about a hundred of us in the group. Oops. I still have the tag on."

I read it before she pulled it off and she snickered.

"No that's not my name that's a name they chose for me tonight. Don't ask me why. My name is Sharon. Sharon Stoetjer, but Sharon will do well enough."

"My name's A.J. Aaron. You smoke cigars often?

"No, ha ha I do *enjoy* them *occasionally* though! Not quite sure why I'm having one tonight though. Someone gave me one for some reason while we hopped and then someone lit it for me." She looked at it as she put it in the ashtray.

The bartender came back with her beer and I paid for it.

"Thank you!" She smiled and tapped my bottle with hers and then sipped on hers while standing there just looking at me.

"Want to sit?" I motioned to get up.

"Oh no no stay please. So how do the wife and kids like your traveling?"

"They don't mind too much as I don't usually travel that much anyway. How did you know I was married?"

"That doesn't matter. I would be here whether you were married or not."

Now I was wondering what she meant by that. I had a strange feeling this was going to be another meeting of another person on the same path. We had some discussion about what we did and what we read and music etc. and found a number of common areas. I told her about my kids and my wife and where we lived. She was a Psychologist going for her MBA, working in a hospital evaluating emergency room cases etc. for psychological disorders. Sounded like a Plant Manager in a few ways to me. Ha ha ha! We had read similar books and listened to similar music. As we talked animatedly, conversation flowed freely and comfortably. After a bit I asked her what she may have meant.

"Earlier you said you would be here if I was married or not. I'm not quite sure what you meant by that."

"Well, sometimes people can tell things about people and I believe there are no accidents. I could feel something about you that drew me to you. Kind of a, 'need to speak to you.' Don't get me wrong, I'm not about to mess up your marriage. I could feel something about you though that told me I needed to speak with you. To meet you."

"Then why can't I feel you? Why aren't I feeling you? That is if I'm thinking what you're feeling is what it is. I guess I can tell you a story and maybe you won't think it's strange."

"Go ahead!"

I proceeded to tell her about how Beth and I met with all the lead up with the dream and the story I wrote and the plane landing at 11:38 and all of it. While I spoke she responded without the slightest bit of surprise being revealed through the entire story. Her intense blue inquiring eyes, with her shifting, tilting, head made me a bit uneasy as I spoke. She seemed to be listening so intently, that I wasn't used to it. When I had finished, I stopped and there was a short silence, as if she waited to be sure I was done, while she looked into my eyes with that same intensity. Then she spoke.

"That doesn't sound strange or unusual. You're not crazy. You're discovering the things that have been hidden that's all. I've had similar experiences and know others who have as well. Don't worry, you're not going crazy. Trust me I'd know! I know what crazy looks like! HA ha ha." She laughed easily from the depth of herself. A powerful yet pleasing laugh.

"Well I guess a Psychologist should know a nut when they see one." I laughed as well but then went back to my question.

"Then Sharon, why can't I feel you if in fact you were feeling me and were drawn to me. From my 'vast' experience with Beth I thought that the feeling of each other was a mutual thing. Am I somehow blocking you out, or is there a wall up I can't get through? I can feel the energy tonight but not you in it."

She looked away a bit as if I caught her off guard. Then she turned back and asked me if she could buy me a beer. I called the bartender over and she insisted on paying for them both when he returned. We talked some more and then realized how long we had talked, and I had not had a chance to talk with my friends, nor her with her friends. I went to find my friends and she went to find hers. Before the night was over we had talked some more and exchanged names, addresses, phone numbers and e-mails and I had met her friends, and she mine.

How could this be? Another one. How would I explain this to Sadie? Well at least I wasn't getting physically involved with these women. Not that I ever had any propensity to do so.

Why couldn't I *feel* her if in fact she could *feel* me. It sure seemed she could feel me the way we communicated and with what she said about why she came over. It was as if she was there to help reinforce what was happening in my life to assure me I wasn't crazy. I was told once by a Freemason* that one Freemason could recognize another and find them in the room. I had asked this person how but they had no explanation and assured me it wasn't from a special handshake, or what they wore, or anything like that.

Now I think I may be seeing what he meant though. She had felt me the way a Freemason might sense another.

It wasn't long after I returned home that I had a dream one night. A dream I had been having before and had forgotten about. I was riding up an escalator in a mall and at the top of the stairs was a woman that was motioning for me to come into her store. It was a book store. Now I recognized her. It was my friend Sharon. I now realized I had dreamt of her before I met her as well. And sure enough, in real life, we exchanged bunches of books with each other through the mail and when we visited each other, either I up there or, she at our house.

*(Freemasonry is a society that has members that can only be admitted by recommendation by other members and a code of death for speaking about its secrets with outsiders. It is said that the Catholics disliked them because they learn what the priests learn. Their knowledge base goes back before organized religions. They are also known for their good deeds and support of charities)

A New Reality

I guess, that was what the bookstore in the dream was saying, and part of what she represented to me. A source of information and reinforcement that what was happening was real.

With Sharon, I didn't have nearly the open connection I did with Beth, but Sharon was astounded at how intuitively accurate I could be with her, even when I was telling her what she may not have wanted to hear. We could connect from time to time, but there wasn't an open door, and it almost seemed as if things were against us being too much in touch as we always had communication problems (technical as well as timing) and problems arranging meetings.

We had some tougher moments, as I sometimes am brutally honest about how I feel and have been known to be somewhat critical, like when we had the frequent trouble establishing communications. I would end up trying to find blame in her for it, when it was totally unjustified, as it was, beyond her control. But that was only a result of my frustration getting the better of me. As it fell out, we ended up remaining good friends, though separated by many more miles than before as she moved from place to place in Europe.

A few of the more interesting connections I'll explain to you here as they truly were amazing to me and helped to validate what was occurring. They also show that Sharon fit into whatever group Beth and I were a part of, which somewhat explains the strange way we met. It also somewhat explains what that Freemason spoke about years ago. These connections follow in the next chapter..

Sharon Connections

The first real connection occurred in a rather strange way in that it involved e-mail. I was dropping a note to Sharon one night online and thought she could use some energy and uplifting as she had been working a couple of jobs and going for her Masters, as well as running a few hours a day to train for a 26 mile marathon for Muscular Dystrophy. She did all this, along with taking care of her two champion show horses, a couple of dogs and a cat. Consequently, she was only getting 3 or 4 hours sleep a night. She seemed to manage it all well but I thought I'd send her some anyway since I felt tired just thinking about all her activity.

Well, I had never thought about sending something like that in an e-mail but I thought, intention is intention, so I finished my note to her, closed my eyes and thought of giving her a hug and filling her with energy. I mentally attached it to the e-mail. I didn't mention it in the e-mail since that might prompt a self fulfilling prophecy of sorts in that she might imagine it. I filled it up and clicked the send key. I thought she might mention it if she noticed it.

A few days later (I never knew when or at what time she might pick up her mail with her hectic schedule) I was at my desk at work after having eaten lunch. I was reading and I got this rush of a feeling of energy again. It was past the time when I had the open channel to Beth, though I would from time to time pick up on her

125

yet. But this felt entirely different. The hum and buzz and electric feeling were there but it didn't feel like Beth. It felt unfamiliar. "Sharon!" I thought. She must have opened my e-mail! I called her at her house and the line was busy. That meant she was either online or on the phone. "It must be her I feel," I thought I sent an e-mail to her and put in the subject, "Get off the phone line and I'll call you!"

I waited a couple of minutes while I felt the electricity then called.

"HI! I just opened your note that said you were going to call. Good to hear your voice!"

"You too! It's been some time. You sure have been busy!"

"I know. But you have to explain something. What did you do to that e-mail you sent a few days ago? When I opened it a couple of minutes ago, right before you sent the one to get off the phone as a matter of fact, I got this rush of energy and felt wonderful all over!!"

"My God! It worked! I don't know how, but it worked!"

"What worked!"

"I sent you energy in that e-mail with my intentions and felt it when I sent it. You obviously felt it when you opened it, and it must have been you opening it that I felt. I felt it when you opened it, and that's why I sent the note to get off the "pewter" so I could call you. I knew it was you opening that e-mail that gave me that feeling.. This is the first time I could feel you. Finally!"

Sharon's power filled voice beamed into my ear, "Well I can feel *you* all right!! Not too bad! Ha ha ha ha…for an old fart! Ha ha ha. This is rather pleasant."

I closed my eyes and felt the energy exchange and knew she was doing the same. Then after a brief pause I heard her speak.

"A white shirt with blue stripes. Is that what you have on? I never saw you in a stripped shirt. You've always worn solids when I saw you."

"Wow! You got it all right. Well Duchess I have to run. I have a meeting in a couple of minutes. Are we still on for your visit?"

"So far it looks like it will still work, but don't be disappointed if it doesn't okay. I can't promise how things are going to go. I know how disappointed you've been with our previous attempts that have fallen through. You know I have done my best to make them happen, but things happen!"

"I know I know and I don't mean to make you feel bad about them but I know I have … Sorry. I guess we just have to let things happen."

"Okay, take care."

"See ya soon."

"Hope so."

Her professional, confident, knowledgeable and melodic voice echoed in my ears until I heard the buzz of the line as the connection ended. Hers was a voice that always made me feel confident and self assured. I guess that was why she did what she did as a Psychologist. She was a natural. I grabbed the folder off my desk, and my tenth, or so cup of coffee and went to the meeting as the wonderful feelings left me to my now heavy feeling physical self.

A New Reality

That was the first experience of connection with Sharon's energy. The next one was rather odd and I wasn't sure at first whether it had happened until I got a confirmation of it that it did. It started one night after dinner when I was doing some I-Chin.

I had gone through the exercises and had accumulated quite a bit of energy as my body was hot and I could feel the Chi flowing through me. For such a non physical exercise it sure did generate heat in me. As I was about to release the energy I thought why waste it. I thought about trying to send it to Sharon and use it to see if I could see where she was.

I stood there, faced in her direction, and closed my eyes. I visualized Sharon as I raised my arms and pointed them in her direction. I asked to see her and imagined the stretch of my arms off to her direction just as in the I-Chin exercise where you imagine a stretch. Then I willed the energy through my arms and fingertips, off to that direction.

I felt the flow of energy as it left me and the cool aftermath that enveloped me as my legs weakened and my body relaxed. A refreshing coolness enveloped me as I tried to visualize what was happening about her with my eyes shut. I sensed that I had found her and made a connection. I felt a rushing feeling like someone hurrying and saw a light green color around me. I wasn't sure what it was, but it was the usual fleeting glimpses I'd get when I went to see where Beth was. From what I could tell, she was hurrying and there was green around her. That was about as far as I could get, since I now had to sit because I felt drained. Maybe she was feeding the horses and getting ready to run? Maybe the green was grass but it seemed to surround her and she was in a hurry. I wasn't sure what it was it was so fleeting.

I tried to call her house but just got the machine. I left a message that I was interested in knowing what she was doing at the time I was doing my thing and that I'd like to compare notes. I didn't get her for a couple of days but when I did it was interesting.

"HI! Good to hear you! What's up!? You spoke about what I was doing at a particular time and date!"

"I did a bit of an experiment here and I need to know where you were and if you could describe it to me."

"Sure. I was at work and I remember that time exactly cause I had to run down to the emergency room. I had to go through this corridor under the ground to get there that I always hated going through. It seemed as if there was something there with me at the time, and since that corridor always spooked me, I looked back as I ran through it and into ER but no one was actually there in the corridor with me. If that was you there, I don't think I'd have been spooked, but like I said I always get spooked there anyway. Does that help any?"

"Hmmm. What color is the tunnel?"

"Green, that ugly institutional green! So what did you do?"

I explained what I had done, and I guess I may have been there, with the hits that there was the green and the hurrying. Due to Sharon's nature and the hectic schedule she keeps, the hurrying is normal for her most anytime. The green? Lots of green around in many places. Maybe a hit, maybe not.

"Maybe a hit."

"Maybe!" She resounded. She was convinced it was. I guessed it could be.

We got up to speed on the latest happenings with each other then hung up. I relaxed on the sofa as I thought it through some more. Sharon's visit to us was approaching, and unless some unforeseen obstacle came in the way of it again, we would have a weekend together to enjoy our strange relationship and our strange connection.

A couple of weeks passed since we spoke, and Sharon was now due to come out this weekend. I hadn't any confirmation though, and I really would like to have known, so I could take a half day vacation on Friday to get the usual chores done around the house so everything would be ready for her on Saturday.

I went out into the front yard and stood with our neighbor and Sadie. I watched the clouds go by in the western sky as the colors just started to change in anticipation of the sunset. I was thinking about how difficult it was for Sharon and me to communicate and was hoping to hear from her soon. As I was watching the clouds I could have sworn I saw the clouds take the form of Sharon sitting at the computer. It was a side view and it showed the monitor and the keyboard with her arms extended and typing. Her profile was immediately recognizable to me. I stood and stared at it as it formed, and then as quickly, dissipated.

Had I imagined it? If not, then she would be online now doing her e-mail and I could possibly catch her. I ran inside and booted up the PC. I signed into my e-mail and checked my inbox. There was one from Sharon. I opened it. It was dated with the date that day and the time was three minutes earlier than the present time. Wow! Whether the clouds formed as they did, which I consider to be **highly** unlikely, or I imagined it as I did that painting in PA, it **was true** that she was online at that very time.

I immediately sent a reply but she was already off line. I did get my answer on the weekend in that e-mail though. The weekend was still on, so the chances looked good she would be out. Was this a coincidence? Maybe.

I don't think the clouds really rearranged themselves for me but there is no reason why my mind couldn't have **perceived** that happening. Why couldn't the electric synapses occur at the proper time to create my perception of that occurring? Now the idea that we may not all perceive things the same is starting to become very probable to me. Does the sky color of blue look the same to everyone? Does food taste the same? How would we know how someone else perceives their environment? Perception is in fact nothing more than just electrical signals interpreted by the brain. But how could she connect to me, to give me that image or, I to her, to capture it? YES, insanity is the only explanation from my logical mind… unless, of course, I'm missing information that I need to answer this. "Please," I thought, "Let me find the information I need to explain this mess!"

A New Reality

Sharon did arrive that weekend. She appeared at my door just after lunch with a smile and a big hug. Of course, she brought the ever present bag of books to exchange and some small gifts for the kids, Sadie, and I, along with a bottle of wine.

There she is! I don't believe it. We did it. The damn communication wall has allowed a leak to pass. "How are you! You look great!" I took the things from her arms and put them on the ground for a good hug. I always take my hugs. I love hugs!

"Uhngh! That feels great! Soooo good to see you!" Sharon said with a deep sincerity and promise of her undivided attention for the weekend. She leaned back as I held her, and she looked at me while she smiled and tilted her head absorbing all sorts of information I'm sure. The way she looked always gave that impression of utter alertness and awareness just sucking the data from the air and everything near.

"Let me get your things." I went down to her car ahead of her and she chased behind me to open the trunk. She took things out as I took them from her and we went inside. I put her things in the visitor's area and we went into the kitchen and got some fresh squeezed lemonade.

"Thanks I'm dying of thirst! There was a NASCAR race today and it tied the traffic up getting out of the state. I was flying after that and I didn't want to stop. Mmm, good, thanks. Show me around?"

"Sure!"

I took Sharon around our house and she, as I said earlier, absorbed everything in each room. Making little noises as she walked such as, "Mmm, Hmm yes Oh my." and so on.

"Sharon, I can't thank you enough for making the trip. I didn't think about it before but now I can imagine it takes a different type of person to come to a married friend's house when the friend isn't the same gender. I mean you and Beth were complete strangers to me and now you're not and you certainly aren't male but you are here."

"Where's Sadie?"

"She's working and the kids are next door playing outside. They'll be here soon."

"I guess most people would think it odd but I don't. That's the problem with a lot of people. They let their notions of what's right and wrong, based on their fears, get in the way. A friend of mine once said you can live your life in love or live it in fear. You pick. I pick love not fear. Why fear what other people think? If people are honest there's nothing to fear is there?"

"I guess not. I don't know if I'd be able to face someone who's not as fearless though. I mean Sadie is an exception, as are you" I motioned to her.

"I guess she is. Your house is very comfortable feeling. Let's see the backyard."

We went around the yard then went back in and Sharon went through all the goodies and books she brought. Then it was my turn to take her through my books so she could refill the bag and take them back with her. By the time we were through Sadie and the kids had returned. Introductions were made and the kids went back to play as Sadie, Sharon and I went on the back deck to sip some lemonade while waiting to cook dinner.

I had the boom box out there and Sharon selected some music. It was during one of the songs that I again felt her really open. I could feel the intense tingle/electric feeling as it radiated out from her while she listened.

"Wow", I said to Sharon as my wife gazed back at me not quite sure what I was "wowing" about. "That song really opens you up!"

"It does every time. I love that song so much!" She said as she now had that blissful look on her face. She knew I could feel her and I now knew why I couldn't before.

"You don't let your shields down very often do you? That's why I couldn't feel you that night we met. You were shielding. Kind of hiding yourself from me. I'm not sure why since you feel just fine."

"You think so? Hmmm." She said as she closed her eyes for the last few seconds of the song. After it ended I could feel the connection dissolve as she came back to her shielded self again.

"That was marvelous!" Then, she changed the subject.

"Hey I have some jewelry for Kara to pick from. I got some semi precious stones and have been playing with making different things with them. I see her in the yard. Kara, Kara can you come here a second?" Sharon called over the railing of the deck to my daughter below. My princess came up and picked out a green malachite pendant in a silver setting.

We had a great dinner, and afterwards we set out to the front yard where it was cooler, and we could see the western sky as the sun went down. Sharon, Sadie and I chatted some more as we listened to music and felt the cooling night air begin to move in. The sky was filled with various clouds and a rumble could be heard in the distance.

"How nice! Maybe we'll get a bit of a storm as it blows through. I love it when it's stormy and I'm somewhere to be able to enjoy it." Sharon commented as she sipped her strawberry daiquiri.

"I don't think we'll get much if we do. It isn't supposed to do too much tonight and it's supposed to be nice tomorrow too." Sadie mentioned to Sharon, as Sharon listened to the now louder rumbling as it moved closer to us. The wind started to pick up and Sharon moved her chair out further into the open as a crack reverberated from the western sky. She closed her eyes again, and once more, I could feel her open as she tried to pull energy from the storm. It felt as if she was, and it was a strong enough feeling that it started to bother me. I was afraid she might actually pull a bolt out of the air the way my skin felt charged and it flowed through me. From the looks of Sharon she was definitely feeling it and probably causing the increase in it.

"Hey enough already!" I said to Sharon as she opened her eyes and smiled as the storm moved closer and the wind picked up. "Crack!" another discharge shot off of heat lightning but this time closer yet. Again I told Sharon, "Enough Sharon! One of these times you're gonna drag a bolt right onto yourself if you're not careful."

I felt the energy close up. She shielded once again and the situation seemed to dissipate itself. Sharon opened her eyes again and brought her chair back as she smiled and picked up her drink again. We talked and the storm went away.

The interesting part about this is, it wasn't more than a week from then that Sharon was in her own backyard as a storm was approaching. She was doing the same thing she was here. Sure enough, she went a bit too far. The lightning hit her garage roof and a tree in her backyard about 30 feet from where she sat. It started the tree and the garage on fire and knocked out her phone and her computer. I saw the burnt remains next time I went to her house in Michigan. She had learnt her lesson from that one, she claimed jokingly.

I had heard of people pulling energy from storms and the electromagnetic field in the air does change during an electrical storm. But that's bullshit right? How can people connect to something like that and not get fried? They say your hair will stand up on your arms before a lightning strike but that's simple electrons from the proximity to the charges and any energy you would get would likely kill you. I never felt energy from a storm like I did until Sharon did that. It was pretty incredible. The fact that her garage got hit a week later didn't surprise me either and it did reinforce that I actually felt what I had felt when she did that at our house, or at least it was a strange coincidence again.

It was when I was up north that my wife Sadie was able to get even with me a bit. I had called her as I always do to check in when I travel. I was filling her in on the trip and so on.

"Yeah the ride was fine. We're going to dinner soon. Not sure if Sharon is gonna join us or not as she's got to work late a bit and then she has a presentation to put together for her Master's class tomorrow."

"Okay, well you guys have fun but I have to tell you something. I met someone."

"Uh oh," I thought, "here it comes."

"That's good. Tell me about it."

I could feel her smiling as she spoke, "She's very cute and she weighs about 14 pounds and I think her name's gonna be Shelby. She's got red and white hair and she's very cute! She looks just like the dog Kara drew the picture of last week. She's at the pound and I've been seeing her but I wasn't sure if we were gonna get her or not. We can get her now though, or tomorrow that is. But I have to get there at two o'clock."

"A dog? Uh well, I guess we should if you think so. I'll have to get an early start to get back in time though. I want to be there when we pick her up and bring her home to the kids."

"That's the idea. Can you get here soon enough?"

"Yup we can. How did you come about this?"

"I'm not quite sure but I had to be at school in 45 minutes, and I knew I didn't have time, but I felt I had to get out to the pound before I went to school. I hadn't gone there in a long time and just had this feeling that I had to. So I ran up there, and sure enough, there she was all huddled up and shaking in the corner of a cage on the bottom. She came right out to me. She had just gotten there less than an hour before me. I knew she would be our dog. I think it's a meant to be kinda thing."

Well, it must have been since that dog fit right in and there was no training needed whatsoever with her. She has been an angel since we got her. She was a mess with raw paws and mites in her ears and you could see every bone in her rib cage but it was like she was meant to be with us. She fit in perfect but she doesn't do a thing without Sadie around. Shelby is her name and she even knows in advance when Sadie is coming home. She stirs about and waits by the door usually 5 to 10 minutes before Sadie gets home. It doesn't matter if it's from the store, or from friends, or where Sadie is coming from, or what time of day or night it is. Somehow those two are connected as well.

I did get to see Sharon that trip but it was for breakfast at the hotel after she had about three hours sleep again. She joined us and we chatted for a bit then she was off to her usual overly busy day as we left early to pass quickly through the plant so I could get back to get the new pooch.

Sharon and I are still friends but with much less contact as she moved to Spain and now to Germany. I was fortunate to have her as a friend as we both learned a good amount about ourselves as we shared our lives from time to time, as well as our books, and music.

Beth and I are still in touch and things were changing for the better there with her.

One of the books that Sharon passed to me shocked me when I read it. Naturally since there wasn't any PhD attached to the authors name or, any science behind it, I was reluctant to take the book to heart at first. Additionally, it wasn't a hardcopy and thus, usually didn't get into my books of merit just because of that. But then, when it was related so closely to what was happening, I had to at least consider it. It was written by David Cousins who it says is an internationally renowned psychic, mystic and healer, though I had never heard of him. Maybe he was famous in Europe, but who knows. This book, <u>A Handbook for Light Workers</u>, was published in 1993 by Barton House, Oxford, England.

In any case I started to read it and on page 16 he said,

"Fourth dimensional reality brings the capacity for us all to be telepathic, aware of inner planes..."

Fourth dimension huh. Okay.

Then he talks about meditation and seeing colors. The colors you need to see are for the level you are currently at. And feeling the energy as it flows into your body. "Okay, that happened to me!" I thought. He continues now on page 32,

"You may feel the heat reflecting in your hands....You may also feel warmth creeping up your body.....and your body may become quite hot." Sounds like my I-Chin and meditations alright.

Then as I moved through the book I got to the part that really hit home. He started to talk about soul mates, reincarnation and all the different aspects of the soul. On page 60 he speaks about the soul's aspect:

"A lot of people think their soul mate is one special person of the opposite sex. But soul mates are the seven main aspects of the soul which result from the soul splitting itself during the downward journey. So, in theory if your soul has split into seven aspects, and all seven aspects have split into their opposite polarities (male and female), you could have 14 aspects of your soul incarnating into earth, each incarnating into a different body during the same Earth time. So you could have 14 soul mates down on earth!

"A twin soul, or twin flame, is the opposite polarity of one of these seven aspects who have split themselves." He continues now into the part that really hit home.

"Therefore the soul prefers to keep each aspect well away from each other. So soul mates are normally spread out around the planet in order to give the soul the multiple permutations within the various time space settings that are appropriate for its needs.

"When someone meets their soul mate it is an event of great importance. The soul's purpose in bringing two aspects of its soul together is to create an energy flow to shift misaligned energy, mainly astral, and to unclog some of the subtle network of energy inputs. This only happens when there is a lot of karmic business to be resolved. *When it does happen, a terrific amount of high frequency energy will result and the two soul mates have a tremendous impact of energy on and in each other's space.* Then, depending on the threshold of each individual aspect, the required change can take place.

"So a meeting of soul mates only happens to those who are sufficiently developed to maintain and hang onto the high frequency energy, who have the courage to change, and are karmically ripe within the essence of their soul life…

"But to meet a soul mate these days is not for personal gratification, or for a mating process to take place. It is more a bringing together for work, mainly on the inner planes, so that the whole soul family can move forward into a much more concentrated essence of what's required.

"Therefore soul mates today really only meet when the vibrations of the soul group move more into harmony and when they have a need of that joint venture, because the age of the individual is over, and the age of the group is now the dominant factor.

"*When you do meet a soul mate you can usually recognize them by the pattern of energy interchange-* which is not always love and joy! *Sometimes though you belong so totally you can swoop in and out of each others bodies with no resistance at all…*

"But it is only when the evolution of the individual soul has reached a pitch where individual aspects can match each other's high frequency energy input, can they start to work together in a concentrated and specific way. As they eventually get very near to each other, working within physical matter through telepathy, through astral alignment, *they will know specifically and on a conscious level what each other is doing.*

"This normally only manifests when they are coming to the end of their earthly cycle."

Earthly cycle in this case meaning earthly reincarnations. Hmm someone a long time ago told me once that I was a very old soul. I had no clue then what that meant. Maybe he was right.

So here is this author writing what seemed to be the exact thing that happened to me. Beth, Sharon, connections, seeing things through Beth and Sharon's eyes, wow. This guy may not be a Doctor or a recognized authority or intellectual figure, but he just described what happened to me!! If I threw away my blinders and what I'm **supposed** to believe to belong socially to our, "normal" society, I can buy in to what he said. I started to throw away my old beliefs. I can't be nuts, this is all *too* coincidental! Thanks for the book Sharon!

Back to Pennsylvania

I had the need to go back to Pennsylvania again with some coworkers. We all went out to dinner together, then after dinner, my friends from work and I met Beth in the hotel lounge and chatted. After a couple hours, as the night was drawing to a close, Beth and I went for a walk to see my picture of the flowers on the wall with the beaten down Angel at the bottom of the vase. Beth had been avoiding it all night, as if she didn't want to know about it, or was scared of it. I suspected something bothered her about that picture because I asked her to go look at it several times on the phone, and she would never tell me she went, or that she'd seen it. She'd change the subject and move on. After a while I stopped asking her about it but tonight I had to see it and show it to her. I had to see it again.

We had said our goodbyes to the people from work and headed down the hall to the conference center.

"Oh Beth don't let me forget, I have a book for you. You have to read what it says. I think I told you on the phone but still."

"Yea about the twin flames? Ha ha ha yea we're real flames all right. Ha ha ha"

We started our way down the long corridor to the conference centers. Beth was substantially better than the last time I saw her but still showed some symptoms on occasion.

"I'll give it to ya later." We continued down the halls as we
spoke. Her arm
linked to mine as we walked.

"Now, did you look at that painting, or picture down the hall
yet!? The one of the
flowers and the Angel crushed at the base? The one I saw before I
met you after I had that dream with the letters of your name?"

"Well, uh."

"You didn't did you?"

I stopped us to look at her eyes.

"Do we have to go there?"

"I have to show you!"

I put her arm in mine again and continue to lead her to the
painting.

"A.J. I have to tell you I did see it." She stops us walking
now and looks into my eyes.

"Isn't it weird?"

"It's not what you said it was."

"Then you saw the wrong one."

I could tell by her look that she was afraid for me to see it. I
took her arm again and we continued. I could smell the stale coffee
as we passed a conference refreshment table still to be cleaned up
and it brings a flashback of the painting to my mind as I remembered
it to be.

We approached the painting and I go up close to it.

"The flowers are the same, but the colors are duller, but otherwise the same

painting but, the vase is plain. No broken Angel."

"They must have changed it!"

"Nope I remember this one here for years. I always liked it. But I asked at the desk anyway if someone changed it. They said they didn't and it's screwed to the wall so it's not likely someone else would."

I couldn't believe it. I turned around and saw the chair I sat in across from it. The phone down the hall, the room we were in. I felt the painting to see if it was in fact screwed to the wall. It was, quite well, none of the corners would even lift.

"I saw it! I know I did."

Beth wrapped her arms over my shoulders from behind as I stared at it in disbelief.

"I know you did and you probably did see what you saw! It's kinda like what the color blue looks like to someone else. How would you know? Like the way I don't know what I look like to you sometimes?"

I turned around to see Beth again.

"An Angel. You would never think I was nuts even if I was would you?"

"Never ever in a million, trillion, gazillion, years, and we've probably known each other that long anyway! Ha ha ha let's go get that book."

Beth was trying to make me feel better but I was feeling insane again.

She looked at me laughing, then consoling me, and kissed me on the lips and hugged me and then gave me her arm to take her.

"You worry way too much."

"The book is in my room. This way."

I took Beth's arm and we crossed into the room wing from the conference center.

"Well, thanks for the wonderful dinner and the great time."

"No problem. A pleasure, I still can't get over how close I feel to you. The folks from work were wondering who the hell you are."

"I think the woman figured us out. She seemed the least affected by it. The other's tried not to show it, but you could tell they were uncomfortable about it. They weren't sure if we were bed mates, or what. Ha ha ha." Beth laughing that deep luscious laugh of hers before continuing.

"They can't even begin to imagine how intimate we really are, and in ways they can't even comprehend. Yet they think you and I would be foolish enough to screw up your wonderful marriage by getting physical."

"Well, ya know I'm startin to get tired of people jumping to conclusions if something doesn't fit their perfect little world of how things are supposed to be. Why is it that a man can't have a woman for a friend without everyone jumping to conclusions!" Pisses me off!"

"Now now. I kinda get a kick out of their antics. You know
we'll probably have
them talking about us for hours before it's all over."

"Probably. Another step on the road of becoming a pink
monkey."

"Pink monkey?"

"I'll tell ya about it later. We're here."

Beth entered the room first while I held the door for her then
let it clunk shut behind us. I went to my suitcase and looked for the
book while Beth took a seat on the edge of the bed. I find the book
and come over to sit next to Beth to show her.

"See, it's a book written by what I would normally call a
nutcase, since nothing is supported in it. But, it describes what's
been happening to us perfectly. So whether it's true, or not who
knows."

I look at Beth as she looks over the book. I can feel the
energy between us begin to build again. Like an electric current
intertwining from both of us. Seems like relaxing can give it the
opportunity to open. Beth looks back up.

"Could be. You never know. Maybe the familiarity of us
comes from us having been in other lives together. Maybe we're part
of the same soul like it says. The part you marked about the leaping
in and out of each others bodies is sure accurate!"

We stopped talking and looked into each others eyes. I ask
her verbally.

"You can feel it can't you."

"Very much so bud. See, maybe this confirms the book is right!"

"Oh come on! Don't make me think I'm even more nuts now. Shit Beth! What am I supposed to do?"

"Exactly what you've been doing. Loving me and letting me love you and know that whatever is the reason for what is happening, and whatever makes it happen, doesn't matter. It happens. We have been given a gift. Be thankful for it."

"I guess. I never had a friend as close as you. It's erie, but you're right. If we have been together forever, and maybe we have., maybe were just parts of the same soul. Maybe we're just a couple of lunatics."

I stood her up and gave her a hug, feeling the energy as it seemed to engulf us both. She leaned back and looked at me. I walked her back to her car and she went home.

After that trip I was confused but, with time, I was becoming more open to all this weird stuff, or at least more accepting, and I decided to do some of my own research. I decided to go to a psychic to see what she might find. She was an aura reader. I never would have believed that psychics or, whatever you wanted to call them, were for real, but she did pretty well, better than I ever would have expected. Here is the first visit to her that I thought you'd find interesting.

The Aura Reader

My hair cutter, Katherine, had told me about an aura reader she had gone to that gave her an accurate reading and balanced her aura for her. She had found all of Katherine's maladies and had then given her a balancing. It sounded like she had done well with it and since I had seen auras myself, for a certain time period in my life; I decided to make an appointment with the woman.

The day came. It was June 12, 1999. The appointment was for ten thirty in the morning that Saturday. I went to Katherine's shop to drop off a couple of articles on Spas for her since she was presently in the process of setting up a new one of her own.

"Hey what did ya do? Come in for coffee again?" Katherine belted out as I dragged my mug into her shop and around the corner to the coffeepot. I put some Irish cream and coffee in it, and went over to Katherine and handed her the articles.

"I saw a couple of articles on day Spas in a magazine and the newspaper and thought you'd like to see them. See, I didn't just come to mooch coffee."

"Oh wow! Thanks. I just went to this one in the paper yesterday. It was a real nice place."

"Sadie said you should skip the golf trips and take spa trips to get ideas for yours. Hey the reason I'm here is I'm going to see Marilyna today, your reader."

"Oh neat! Call me after and tell me about it okay?"

"I'll do that. Did my name come up in your reading or have you told her about me? I called from work and made the appointment and since there are so many trunk lines her caller ID wouldn't show anything. I only gave her my first name and I'm taking off my twenty-year watch and my ring so she doesn't have any of that to draw clues from. No logo shirts or jackets and so on. So if you haven't said anything to her she should be without any clues about me."

"Nope. I didn't say anything to her. Haven't talked to her since."

"Great! Well, I better get going, my appointment is for ten thirty. See ya."

"Okay, see ya later darlin."

I stepped out into the sunlight and got in the car. I sipped some of the coffee, lit a cigarette and started the car. The music kicked in and I was off. It was a gorgeous day. The temperature was about eighty degrees now and with all the windows down, the air was refreshing.

I drove east on the freeway for about ten minutes and exited where Marilyna had told me. I followed her directions off the Saturday page of my weekly planner. I found her street in the quaint town by the shore with its cottage type homes with flowers in the yards and birds singing. I was fifteen minutes early so I decided to drive around the neighborhood a bit.

The shaded streets were cool and pleasant. The perfume of fresh cut grass filled my nose and lungs as I passed down a street that had been maintained with its original brick paving. I found a village green complete with a large gazebo and a war memorial. There were a number of old oak trees, whose shade looked inviting, to finish my coffee and have a smoke under. I parked the car on the street and walked over to an oak that must have been a hundred years old at least. I sat beneath its long leaf covered arms on the cool grass.

A couple of squirrels were having a game of chase across the lawn. I drank the rest of my coffee and finished my smoke then closed my eyes and went through my chakra colors. I imagined each as a disc in its position on my body in a line from the bottom of my torso to the top of my head. Red, orange, yellow, green, blue, fuschia, white. The green seemed to respond by showing me a brilliant green before my third eye as I spun it. I could feel the energy in the given position as I went through them. The other colors were present as I went through them but today the green stuck out. I pulled some energy from the earth and dropped my heart rate and breathing some to relax.

I was a little nervous about what this woman would say or find so this relaxation helped. I opened my eyes and looked at my watch and had two minutes left before the appointment. I took the watch off and put it in my pocket and took off my ring and did the same. I got up and went to the car and drove down the street. I arrived right on time to find her standing out in front of her house.

"Good morning Marilyna. I'm A.J.," I said as I approached her.

"Nice day huh? Excuse the midgies. We had a ton this year, as you can see," she said as she walked toward the door and motioned at the heap of little dead midgey flies she had swept in a corner on the ground.

"Yeah you sure did get a bunch. That's one of the disadvantages of living by the lake, but it's worth it I bet. I love this area. The beach is super too."

"You're right. I love it here. I've been here for a year and a half so far and it's a great place to live. Can I get you something to drink?" she asked once we entered her living room.

"Sure, a glass of water would be great." I said as she went to the kitchen.

I stood in her living room and looked around a bit. The ceilings had blue crown moldings and the house had a Victorian charm to it. The mantle on the fireplace had a barrage of angels on it. There were more spread throughout the room. A couple of teddy bears sat in frozen wonderment, gazing out from the circular end table. Candles of all shapes and sizes were scattered in the room, large pillars and small votives. Candle covers with stars cut in them and tapers. A book on Yogi (No not the bear or the baseball player) was on the coffee table along with a tile-like coaster that had an I-Ching symbol on it. I sensed no smell what so ever here. No incense, flowers, perfume or food smells. Very neutral. Not even anything emanating from the candles though they weren't lit anyway.

She led me into the dining room where we sat opposite each other at the table. She removed a piece of white, standard, eight and a half by eleven paper and handed it to me. As she reached for a candle and lit it, she gave me these instructions.

"Take the paper between both of your palms and hold it for a while sending energy into it. Then, when you are done I want you to pass it over the candle flame very close so that it leaves a residue on it. I'll then use that side to read from."

"Okay." I responded as I held the paper and sent energy into it. I thought about different things to see if she would pick up on them. In particular I thought about Beth and pictured her and I thought about Sharon and pictured her. I wanted her to find these two and see what she said about them.

Then, I just sent energy into it with out much further thought. When I was done I started moving it over the candle. I moved it closer until I could see the soot depositing on it. I circled the flame and ran it thoroughly back and forth as I felt her watching me. I was very suspect of any readers, as this wasn't possible, of course. I knew she had no clues to go by with me though since I wasn't giving any. I was hoping I could feel her energy, and then I'd be more comfortable with whether she spoke the truth, or not, but I still couldn't get that sense back on command, or she might be like Sharon, shielding most of the time. When I was done I passed the paper to her.

"Okay, very good. Hmm. There is a great deal of pain and a hard time that you have had recently. I can see a large, very large amount of people about you. I think there has been something that has happened in your job. A demotion or reduction in responsibilities in some way. But you are much healthier and happier now for it. You used to get ill easily toward the end of that previous job and now you are better. A large amount of people. Did you have a large amount of people working for you?"

"About two hundred and fifty or so. Now I don't have anyone but myself."

"Yes, this change was a good thing for you. Something you needed."

Well, I thought, she is off to a good start. She nailed that one right on the head. Not a demotion but definitely a reduction in responsibilities though I would be a grade level higher. Then she went into a different subject. She seemed to jump around a lot from subject to subject sometimes returning to one or another. The next thing she said was,

"Angelo, his name is Angelo and he is wearing a yellow tee shirt right now. He is in a yard working. Maybe a yard worker or landscaper. He has vivid green eyes. Yes very green. He is a guide of yours. Do you know him?"

"He is here now? On this earth? In human form?"

"Yes, he has not passed if that is what you mean. Do you know him?"

"No, I don't. Don't know who he could be."

"Vivid green eyes. Angelo. He is a guide of yours."

"Okay."

"Music. Hmmm. I see many instruments about you. Very many. You have a love for music. It affects you deeply. Stirs your

154

soul. It is a very powerful force in your life. I see a woman. Very pretty. She has pretty reddish brown curling or wavy hair, pretty hair, a very good attitude, a winning attitude to overcome things. She has a very musical voice with a musical sound to it. Oh yes! She loves to dance too. She just <u>loves</u> to dance. This person is good for you. She is a good influence. Do you recognize her?"

"Recognize her? I think you know her well enough to know her full name even. Yes, she is a friend of mine and her name is Beth."

"I can't always see a name. Sorry. There is the word sister here. You don't have a sister do you?"

"No I don't."

"Then you were raised Catholic and she was a nun. You don't consider yourself Catholic now. She has passed on. She was very fond of you when you were in the Catholic school. She always made a big deal over you when she saw you. She has her hand on your head as she did before. She is here now and she was with you through the dark time you went through. She is still watching over you. She has passed and is a guide for you. Do you know whom I speak of?"

"Yes, that is Sister Elizabeth. She called me, "church mouse" and, "little angel". She would always touch me on the head when she saw me."

"There is a hooded figure. A monk, or priest, or something of that sort that would dress in a hooded garment. He is a guide of yours also. He isn't here now but he is a guide. There is also an angel guide and Saint Theresa. They are all guides of yours as well."

I wasn't sure about the hooded figure but I had seen an angelic figure repeatedly in my meditations. The figure was Angelic in the sense of riveting beauty and androgynous appearance, with golden hair and radiant eyes and skin. The hooded figure could be the reason for my new interest in the Celtic and Wiccan areas.

"I see a swimming pool and children's voices. No adults around. I see the number three. I don't know what it means in relation to that. Three days or weeks or something else but three. It is some sort of event you are at. A swimming pool."

I didn't know what that could be about but after it happened I remembered what she said. She was actually warning me but wouldn't say there was a danger in that it could come true as a self-fulfilling prophecy if she did. What happened was a week later at a friend's house. In the back yard the three of Mark's kids were playing. The two-year-old had gotten away from the other two and had made her way up the steps to the pool deck and had fallen in. She didn't know how to swim. Her brother fortunately noticed her. She fell in trying to get on a raft and he ran over and went up and yanked her out. That was the pool with no adults around. We were there not aware that the pool gate was open and the little girl had gotten up there. We thought she was with the other two.

Marilyna now looked up from the paper and looked around me. She said I had an enormous amount of energy. My aura was a vivid green. It had a couple of chinks in it but was strong and healthy. She said,

"The chinks are no big deal. Everyone has a couple of them. It is a strong and healthy aura. The green signifies growth and health."

After she said that she went back to the paper with a convinced, self satisfied, look on her face because of what she had seen about me. She continued with the reading as I took notes. I wanted to see if I could affect a change in my aura that she could see. I pulled energy from the ground and sent it up into my aura trying to push it up and make it stronger yet as I imagined the green energy flowing out. She continued reading the paper as I did so.

"The book, "Conversations with God" influenced you. Hmm. A woman with short hair that curls at the bottom. A break in this, a wall between you. You are having a difficult time communicating with her. It is difficult for you to communicate with her. There is some sort of a wall. You need to rise above it. You need to rise up to her. She has, how should I say it? Please don't take offense but her shape is somewhat rounded at the bottom. Sort of thin on top and rounder on the bottom a pear type of shape. Do you know who I describe?

"Yes I do."

I thought a bit as she started to look above me now. She had described Sharon and there was a wall of sorts in our communications. We even scheduled times to talk on the phone and it would fall through. Even our e-mails were not completely free of problems. We both greeted every communication success as a victory. Marilyna now looked at and above me.

"My…oh my! You are, your, uh, your energy is leaking everywhere! Yes, you do have a lot of energy. Very powerful!"

She looked about me as she continued with her eyes squinted, and her face showing the look of surprise and awe.

"The field is full of vivid green and its spinning and it's like a, uh, spiraling out of you. It's a vortex as it comes out. Amazing! I don't think I've ever seen that happen like that before. You leak energy and should wear dark colors to help prevent that."

"I feel more comfortable when I wear a black shirt or black jeans. I only started that recently. For some reason it became appealing to me."

"That's right. Why do you think priests wear black? It is for that reason. You recognized that need now as you've grown. That's good." She continued.

"Vacationing in the fall. I see dolphins all around. Are you going some where that has dolphins there, for vacation, in the fall?"

"Not that I'm aware of." I responded at the time. Some time later though I remembered that when we went to my brothers last fall, as we probably would do at Thanksgiving this year, my sister in law had a lot of dolphins in the house. She collected them. Wooden ones and clay etc. I guess I'll find out what the significance of this was if we go. She didn't say anymore about it now though.

"Well, where ever you are there are a lot of dolphins around that I see. That recent change for you at work was much needed for you. You have two children a boy and a girl. The one has a reptile associated with him. Does he own any?"

"No he doesn't."

"Then it is a sign of his nature. The reptile is a snake. It shows he is capable of taking care of himself and not dependent on others. A self-sufficient nature. This is different for the girl. She needs more help emotionally sometimes." Accurate again, she continued on.

"A dam?, A D A M? Adam? He passed as a child, he has freckles and black curly hair. He is very playful but shy. He is here, oops, he ran off into the living room. He was to your left. Do you know him?"

"No I don't." I replied as I tried to feel him but couldn't. I later thought it might have been someone I knew that killed himself after killing two other friends. He was a playful person but was about nineteen or twenty years old, not a child, when it happened. He had curly black hair and freckles. His initials were DAM.

"A heart… A heart was stomped on. I see that as part of that time period when the changes were in process at work. Someone's heart being stomped on. Not sure what it means. But a heart was crushed."

I thought to myself that yes, Beth's heart was crushed. She was in the hospital for nine days and they could find nothing wrong to give her those pains in her chest. I always knew it was a broken heart from the relationship she was in the midst of dealing with at the time.

"I keep seeing a flash of some sort. Some kind of energy an electrical kind of flash that opened you. It happened to bring you to this transition. It was a flash of energy and now you see things very differently. It was the beginning of your changes. You view things very differently now."

"Yup," I thought. That was the connection that Beth and I had initially and the I-Chin energy before. That was the flash. It felt electrical almost.

"There is a chimney that needs cleaning, or has some sort of obstruction. I can see the flow going backwards in it. It is going down instead of up. A kink or something, an obstruction from the top forcing it back down. If you have a chimney I would check it at the top."

I didn't think much of it at the time but I got home and looked at the top of our chimney to see if the cover came off but it hadn't. I didn't clean it because it was too hot outside to do that job now. I'd rather do it in the fall. The following Monday at work though our Plant Engineer, Tom, came into my office. They were having a problem with a braze furnace in the plant, but couldn't figure it out and involved him to help. He came into my office and started,

"I don't get it. There is no negative pressure back there yet the one end of the one braze furnace is backdrafting. I never remember it doing that with positive pressure do you? Even with the pusher fans on in the south wall it still does it. The other flue is okay though as is the other furnace."

"That does sound weird," I responded and then remembered what Marilyna had said. Then I took Tom and we went to check what it was. We walked to the back of the plant to talk to the operator and look at the symptoms. Sure enough, the flue was defying the laws of physics, or so it seemed. So I had to check what Marilyna had said.

"I'm going on the roof," I said.

"It's pouring out!" Tom responded.

"I have to see what it looks like up there."

I went through the plant to the back and up the stairs to the roof, then climbed up the ladder to the upper roof over the braze furnaces and the plating department. The roof was covered with a few inches of water, and as I looked at the four flues from the furnaces, I noticed the problem. The one that was back drafting had steam lazily coming out of it. There is never any steam coming from those flues, just 2100 degree heat. Three were operating normally but the one that was back drafting had steam coming out. Evidently, the water on the roof was leaking into the flue through a chink in it and creating superheated steam. The superheated steam caused an increase in pressure, which would then cause a back draft down to the bottom as well as a release of steam from the top. The steam was pressurizing the flue. I went back down.

I saw Tom and his engineer at the furnace again.

"Marnega, when the roofers get to that part I want to have the flues checked for leaks and redone. I think the southwest flue has something letting water into it. When the water drains from the roof the problem will go away until it rains again. The water is pressurizing the flue with steam and causing the backdraft."

"That makes sense. I'll let you know when the roof is opened up there. Thanks!" Marnega responded.

So she was right about the flue too.

She continued, "Boats everywhere. You have boats all around you. Are you a boater?"

"No I'm not."

"Hmm. There are boats all around you, all sorts, for some reason. That's all."

I didn't have any idea what the significance of this was but I did later on. About two weeks later I was on vacation in Connecticut and I went down to my friend's boat. We stayed the night on the boat, and when we went on our way for the trip, I suddenly remembered what she had said about being surrounded by boats. We were pulling out of the Mystic River and boats were all around us.

I said to my friend Kev, "Surrounded by boats. She said I was surrounded by boats."

"What's that?" Kev asked.

"Oh nothing. The reader said I was surrounded by boats, that's all."

I told him about the swimming pool and the chimney already. So now I was on the alert for something that might happen. As we made our way out further Kev spoke up as he throttled back the engines.

"Look at that! The port engine has lost oil pressure and overheated and now it's stalled. That's a new engine too!"

I looked at the gauges and sure enough the temperature was pegged and now Kev couldn't get a restart.

"I guess it's a good thing we didn't try for Montauk this year. It would have been rough getting stuck with one engine half of the way there," Kev commented.

I remembered the previous year we were out. It was similar to today with a light breeze but today had a strong wind. Last year we had six-foot waves coming back and it wasn't fun with *two* engines. I couldn't imagine it with only one. I guess this was what she was talking about with all the boats.

She had finished her readings and asked if I had any dreams I wanted her to discuss. I told her about some of my dreams and she was able to find meanings in them similar to the meanings I had determined.

Other than her telling me to continue to make space for myself to be alone, and continuing to meditate and listen to my intuition, that was about it. She told me of some metaphysical classes she knew of, if I was interested, and we parted company for now.

So what happened with this reader? She may have coincidentally hit upon some things that triggered my mind to make an association and give some credence to her abilities. The weirdest of all to me is the way she supposedly saw my aura change into the green vortex as I consciously attempted to make it change. One, that she could see it, and two, that I could change it. What would make her think I was doing that, when she had no reason to. It's not like my face contorted from the effort.

So here I am again in a position with little to pose as answers other than multiple dimensions and lots of space between electrons and protons creating the illusion of solidity. But how can any of that tie to someone's intentions, or thoughts, creating, or perceiving, some other reality?

I can now see why what happens in the next chapter is no longer something impossible to me. I can see how the things that led to this occurrence might have happened. All those strange events that precipitated this, (figuratively speaking of course) were rain that fell upon us, and changed us forever. Especially obvious though, were the changes that happened to my friend, Beth.

Again, I needed more answers. Well, as fate or something would have it, I came across more information. This time it came from a person who seemed to be quite an authority in the field. It was a hard copy as well, not a paperback!! My silly prejudice was satisfied. It shed some light on how people like this aura reader might be able to do such a thing, as well as how our intuition might pick things up. But first you must hear a little about the author.

His name is Evan Harris Walker. He is the founder and director of the Walker Cancer Institute. He has made major scientific contributions in astronomy, physics, neurophysiology, astrophysics, psychology and medicine. He has a Ph.D. in physics and has published more than a hundred papers in scientific journals and popular magazines and holds a dozen patents. He is intimately familiar with the workings of our brain and mind and the physics that support it. He takes us from Newton to present day in the book, and reveals his theory of how consciousness exists, and how our will, or intentions, can affect everyday life through Quantum interactions with our surroundings. A true thinker, and great mind of today, and on top of it, he writes most eloquently.

I have included a more detailed description of his book in the appendix for those interested in the details (I highly recommend taking the time to read it as well) but basically he has said that our brains are set up to function through quantum physics. Without the leap of quantum physics there is no consciousness, no synapses to create consciousness. There are two data streams in our brain. One is 5 million bits per second and is our normal sense processing stream and thought stream. Then there is a "will" stream, as he calls it, that is 50,000 bits per second and this is what connects us to other people and creates change. The problem is, the normal processing is such a large stream, versus the will stream, that it gets drowned out. When the normal stream can be reduced the will stream can come into play (through meditation, or focus, on the will stream).

Now I was beginning to believe. I was not crazy!!! My sanity has been salvaged from the quagmire of our society's paradigms. We have a brain capable of allowing the connections to occur. The perceived world is simply that, what we perceive. There is a lot more to be perceived but most people never get to, or never allow themselves to. After reading this book, more than once, I felt I had finally made some sense of my predicament. Then, as things moved on, I also found a reason for meeting Beth.

A Miracle?

"There are only two ways to live your life. One is as though nothing is a miracle. The other is as though everything is a miracle." --Albert. Einstein

Beth told me how she was gaining weight. Something she couldn't do if she tried before (even with the six-pound pound cakes I'd bake and send her). This weight gain was a good sign. The signs continued to get better.

Little did we know, this was just the beginning of a miracle. As time went on Beth showed improvement more and more. Her weight went from one hundred fourteen pounds at five foot 9 to one hundred and forty five pounds. She had to get new clothes and was now complaining that she would have to start dieting soon if this kept up. Of course she laughed at this fact, since that was a dream, after having MS for the last twenty two years and being just a wisp of a being at her height.

Let me define "miracle" for you. Basically it is usually thought of as having "divine intervention" as Webster says in definition number 1, but it also has the meaning of being "an unusual event, thing or accomplishment" as Webster defines it in definition number 2. I like to think of a miracle as anything that falls outside of normal probability. Winning a lottery can be considered to be a miracle as the odds are quite against it. Well, the odds of a reversal of MS are a miracle no matter how you look at it. Did it reverse itself? The doctor said it seemed to be that but that was all. In any case she was getting better and we were all happy for it.

As time went on and her fatigue diminished, her attention to focus on things improved, her voice never lapsed in conversation anymore. She didn't speak quietly any more since she didn't hear herself as if she were speaking too loudly though she wasn't. The heat didn't get to her as badly as it used to. In addition, she had stopped taking *all* of her meds. Then she went to her next check up in six months.

When she went to see her MS neurologist again, he noted her improved condition and he set her up with an MRI to see the state of her myelin sheaths and her brain. The myelin sheaths are what insulate the nerves that carry the signals for motor responses and so on. The fact that they get damaged from the auto immune disorder of MS is what causes the symptoms.

The MRI was able to reveal the extent of the damage to the nerves in the brain. Or at least that's how I understood it. Beth went for the MRI and waited for the results. She knew she was better because of the way she felt but wasn't thinking about a good MRI.

It was May and I was riding in my car with the windows down. Music was playing in the car as I headed home from work. My mind is finishing its closure of the day as I get interrupted. I stopped at a red light and sniffed the air. Yes, it's the perfume. I look around for a source and the light changes. As I drive it persists. It isn't leaving me. I sniff my shirt, as if that would be the source, but I know where it's really coming from. It's Beth. Something is up. I feel for it and realize the news is good, she is excited and I know it is her. "I'll have to call her after dinner," I think to myself.

I get home and enter the kitchen where Sadie is getting the last things into the dining room for supper.

"Hey sweetie!" I lean and kiss her as she turns to have me kiss her on the lips.

"Hi sweetie! Good day?"

"Okay. Just got a whiff of Beth again. Been a long time since that happened. Seems to be something good this time. Gonna have to call her after dinner."

"Yea you two haven't been connecting like you used to."

"I think our purpose of meeting is probably fulfilled, or close."

"Plus, I kinda gave it up so to speak. Wished it away. It got to be too much for me."

"You did? Why!? It was a gift."

"Not inside my head. It was a battle."

"You need to try again."

"I'll use it when I need it. I still use it sometimes but I don't have an open connection to Beth like I did. It opens when it needs to though."

The phone rings and I answer it

"Hello?"

"That's all just hello? Didn't you hear me?"

"Yea yea on the way home. I caught a whiff of your perfume, and felt something good going on. What's happening?" Sadie watches on as I speak.

Beth is in her apartment. I see her in my mind as she looks exceptionally well. She speaks smoothly and fluently without any sign of the previous MS related symptoms. I imagine her full of energy as she paces the floor, with no limps or drags of her feet, talking on the phone.

"Well, you know how I have been getting better. No more meds except for the one shot. Gained weight. More energy. My speech and so on."

"Yea, yea c'mon."

"Well, I went to my neurologist today to get the results of my MRI. He said I'd been touched by an Angel. He wouldn't even read the results to me! He had *me* read them cause he'd never seen anything like it before."

"Yea yea and?"

"You're so impatient! Anyway. The report said that there was no brain atrophy, no evidence of Myelan sheath degradation. It classified as a perfectly normal brain scan! Like someone who doesn't have MS would have."

"NO SHIT! NO MS!! That's great!" Sadie calls out to her leaning into the phone.

"Hurray! Congratulations Beth!"

"No he says I'll always have MS."

"So this is a remission?"

"No not a remission. Remissions don't have changed MRI's."

"Then it's gone."

"He says no, that MS never goes away, but sure it looks like that. I mean I still have some symptoms time to time, but not like before. This brain scan shows why." I could tell Beth picked up the report, and was waving it as she talked.

"I called the maker of my meds and they said they never heard of this before either from *any* of their patients. I think I had a miracle bud."

"I think you did. Did they make sure it was your report?"

"Yea yea. That was the first thing I asked! Date and time, comparison to old ones yea, it's mine!"

"Wow. That's awesome. I guess something did happen that day. I guess there was a reason for us getting together."

"The reason continues bud. I'm not giving you up." Beth says matter of factly.

"I didn't mean that, and I hope you never do. That would devastate me. But this gives our meeting a greater purpose than making each other feel good see?"

"I know. Always looking for answers. That's my bud. Okay bud. I gotta make more calls. Love ya."

"You too, see ya."

Sadie looks at me as I hang up the phone and then she starts in on me.

A New Reality

"Wow! See, you never know what the reasons for things that seem out of place are. See all the good that came from this? What if I did get jealous? Beth may never have gotten better."

"And maybe it just happened on it's own, and we were just doing our thing while it did."

"You amaze me! I believe what happened more than you, and you're the one that it happened to. Will you ever stop doubting?"

"I doubt it. Ha, ha, ha."

I gave Sadie a big hug, laughing.

Beth ended up calling the provider of her MS drug to see if there were any other reports like her. They had never heard of such a thing happening either. So it seemed, by all definitions, that a miracle (however you may like to define it) had in fact occurred (by whatever mechanism you may believe caused it).

What could in fact have caused it? Could the cause be, The Lady of Lourdes or the quantum connection from the energy resident there, or through a quantum connection with higher consciousness (The Lady's?). Could Beth's active will channel have caused it by her controlling her underlying intentions? Maybe through mine and others loving intentions for her? They say that people who are ill get better quicker when someone is praying for them then when someone isn't. Maybe it was a random occurrence, a coincidence. You decide for yourself. You don't need anyone to tell you the answer. You decide. The observer creates the reality remember? So you get to pick your reality. You decide. The way you view this happening is the way you will view the world and thus, the way you will experience the world. You always do get to decide, whether you think about it, or not. If you decide not to think about it at all, well then, that's your decision and your reality. But, you always get to decide.

It's nice to decide isn't it? Kids like to decide which cookie and what flavor. Adults like to decide what carpeting and what shirt etc. Why then, do we always let others decide for us? Why let others say how things should be, what the rules are for us, and what we can, or can't, accomplish. Yes, you decide what happened to Beth and shape your world accordingly by doing so. The way you observe it, is how it is, that we know for sure. Physics has proved that for us when the observer is now known to affect the outcome of the experiment. Or maybe we just observed physics to prove that for us. Whatever, you choose, think, ponder, feel, and choose.

The Winds of Change

I walk past Brad's desk and notice it's considerably cleaner than normal. So clean it doesn't look like his desk. I pass out the door to the plant and see him at the other end some 400 feet away. I think to myself, "What has gotten into you?" His form jerks around and faces me from the other end and he starts toward me. I meet him in the middle of the plant.

"Hey boss! What's up?"

"You tell me. I went by your desk."

"Oh that. Yea. I was hoping I'd see ya. As I said before, it would be time for me to move on soon, now is the time. The universe is weird that way."

"Quit the universe crap."

"I told you before. The catalyst isn't needed anymore, you're on your own. Your Plant Engineer, my boss, let me go today. 10% reduction the GM wanted."

"What!? He doesn't get to say."

"Hang on, hang on. It's supposed to be that way. I get a small severance and a good recommendation. Don't take it out on him; he's doing what he's supposed to.

"Getting rid of pink monkeys eh. You scare him."

"Yea, you do to, but he can't get rid of you. It's supposed to be this way. Just try to not be a pink monkey while you have this job

174

as your only means of financial support, and don't loose faith. The world you are learning about is much bigger than the one you were in before. Don't let it go. Use it."

Brad puts his coffee on the floor and gives me a hug as I struggle to not fall over from the discomfort of this in the middle of the plant. Brad backs away, his tear filled eyes behind the thick lenses.

"You can always call me for a beer."

"I will, I will, Thanks for all your help. Take care my friend."

Brad turns and heads for the door as I watch him leave the plant floor to the office. The Plant Engineer Tom comes marching over to me.

"I know, what the fuck I am doing!? I had to get rid of him. While you were on your trip they asked everyone to reduce 10%. He's the newest guy."

"Remember Tom, I can tell if you're lying. You learned that the other day. You got rid of him because you can't stand him that's why, because he scares you. You were happy to have the opportunity. Don't lie to me about the reason."

He stared at me not knowing how to respond. He knew I wouldn't accept a lie.

"Uh, maybe he wasn't one of my favorites, but..."

"Stop. Stop. Stop. It doesn't matter. It's supposed to be this way. He told me he was leaving a couple weeks ago."

"He couldn't have. He didn't know till today."

"Trust me. He did! He knows a lot more than you can imagine. It's okay, I'm not angry."

"Now I know your nuts!" The Plant Engineer leaves and a couple of my supervisors stop by. Darek smiles a mischievous smile.

"Hey boss. What number am I thinking of? Tom doesn't like the way you got into his head the other day."

I give him a dirty look and he laughs.

"Don't give me any shit, or you'll regret it trust me."

"Okay boss."

Pink monkey now. Shit! I must be nuts. Gotta get back to the old me. Gotta put this stuff aside. Stop the connections or I'll be labeled insane. Why did I have to tell Tom I knew he was lying to me the other day. Then to top it off I tell him exactly what the truth was. Dumb, dumb, dumb. I was making a pink monkey of myself and now I have all the supervisors believing something Tom fed them. Great! I have to stop this connection crap.

I was beginning to get fed up with the whole job of running a plant 24/7 at double the size it was when I started. With no options for developing a management level to be able to split the plant in two functional areas so we could transition to a structure to handle the now double size of the plant, I felt it was becoming a loosing battle. In addition, I felt my learning was done in this area after 9 years of it. It appeared it was time to create a change.

I had begun to research liquidating all our assets and getting a place in the Poconos. It would buy me three years at our current standard of living before I'd need to find income again. After that I could teach in Pennsylvania if need be. Maybe I could get this story written in the meantime. I also had a number of head hunters calling with 25% higher paying jobs than I had at the time, but all would require relocation, as well as the rebuilding of a network and political support wherever I went (reality spoke clearly that this was how things worked and I had learned how to live in that environment though it wasn't the most enjoyable of options). I was trying to feel out my options but getting no good strong direction out of my gut. Logic could support any option in a number of ways, financially or otherwise. I was stuck in the mire of indecision. Ironic. I get to decide too, just like in the last chapter when I asked you to decide, and now I couldn't do it.

I finished dinner one night and went out to the front yard to sit and have my coffee. I took my briefcase and reread some of the headhunters' correspondence; I did a phone interview with one a few minutes later. I looked some more at my numbers on the Pocono option. I was still stumped. I was frustrated and lost because I wasn't sure what to do. This wasn't me. I always knew what to do and went about it. If I didn't have a good logical reason to do something, then I relied on my gut instinct and went from there. That wasn't even working here. I needed a way to come to a decision or I would wallow in the muck of indecision until I drowned.

I took out the picture of my buddy Beth from the briefcase. I looked at it and thought about how screwed up things were for me and about how weird the last few months had been. Was I going insane? I didn't know. I never went insane before. Is this what it felt like? Was this a nervous breakdown? I didn't think so, I wasn't broken. I was just at a loss for an answer on which way to go.

Basically I had two main choices. One was take action, the other one was take no action, throw my oars in the water and see where the boat took me. I had read about such a thing being beneficial at times but I never did such a thing. Relinquish control to fate? Unheard of!! Yet my gut told me nothing and neither did my brain, to direct me at this time. I stared at my buddy's face and felt her love and understanding in her picture. I could almost feel myself connecting to her the way I had before.

I thought to myself, "If this stuff we have is real, and not imagined by me, call me. I need to speak to you now and I need you to hear me call you now. Set me straight and prove to me again that what happened with us is real. If you do that, then I'll know the truth and I'll listen to my own inability to have a decision in this matter. I'll make the decision to do nothing. If you call, I'll take the chance and throw the oars from the boat, and let it drift.

Well, I hadn't spoken to Beth in some time and the chances of her calling me in the middle of the week were highly unlikely. We usually spoke on weekends unless there were issues that needed to be discussed, or unless she wasn't feeling well, and I wanted to check in on her. The constant open line between us mentally, was not there anymore like it was on a daily basis previously. So, after I sent my mental message, I sat in the yard, did nothing, thought nothing, and drifted.

It wasn't very long when the portable phone rang next to me. I answered it.

"A.J. Aaron."

"What? What do you mean A.J. Aaron. It sounds like you're at work. You must be screwed up! What's the matter? I was at my Grams when I got a sense you needed me to call and I figured I'd go home and call you. So here I am. What's the matter bud?"

"Ha ha ha this is incredible. I guess I have to throw the oars in the water. Thanks bud. This stuff is for real. Incredible, but real."

I told her my story and how she helped me make the decision to do nothing and feel good about it. Well, I was glad later that she helped me by calling then, or I would have gone in another direction. A direction of taking action and then, I would have missed arriving at my plateau. The plateau in my dreams that would be there after the rain went away so I could scale it and meet my friend that was there already.

It didn't take long for the winds of change to sweep through our place at work. It happened fast when the division had huge adjustments and variances in all the plants. The metal plants alone had lost close to two million dollars in the past few months on adjustments and they were running somewhere around 20-30 percent. These were unheard of numbers, unreal numbers, and terrible numbers. My plant alone supposedly had three hundred thousand dollars in unfavorable variance, and the accountants were being nice by only booking one hundred and fifty thousand and they couldn't give me any detail to support it.

A New Reality

One day the staff had a meeting. One of them left the divisional operating statement on the copier. I wasn't privy to that information, but was interested to see if the adjustment problems applied to all plants, not just mine. It sure did. In ten minutes I had gone through the operating statement and it was obvious to me that plants couldn't generate those numbers on their own. There was a problem somewhere else. Plants are like machines and it takes a lot to make them change their ratios this much. A lot of concerted effort, or in this case, a lot of messed up numbers.

I no sooner finished analyzing it when my boss came in and told me about the problem I just analyzed and asked me if I knew what was wrong. I told him it wasn't a problem with the plants obviously, and there was some sort of system problem that generated these numbers. I couldn't imagine what, but they were there as these numbers weren't possible. His face lit up and he said,

"Can you be in the meeting in ten minutes, and go through your reasoning to the whole staff?"

"Of course," and I did. It was well received and after the meeting a friend on the staff told me that they had recommended me to resolve the problem.

"I told them that the only person that knew enough of what was going on was you, and that you should solve the problem."

"Oh thanks a lot! How am I supposed to do that. That's a full time job for quite a while and I have a plant to run."

"Don't worry about that." He said, "We'll figure it out."

"Well thanks for your confidence, Anton. I appreciate the good words but I don't know how we're gonna do it."

"It'll be fine. Don't worry."

Little did I know that some of my intentions for change were coming about and quite rapidly at that. My friend Sharon had told me about writing down my intentions very clearly on a piece of paper and keeping it. Coincidentally, I had done that just a couple of weeks before this. Some of the things I put in there were to have time to think and reflect on my day, have more time for my family by not working weekends, be present at home by not taking work home in my mind or getting phone calls at night, having time at work to think and plan and set my own schedule, just to name a few.

Well, the wheels of change rolled right to my door. In a few days I was called into the General Managers office. My boss was there. The General Manager started.

"A.J., I called you in here because the division is in trouble and we need your help. You have a great understanding of how our systems work and as you know, we have a huge problem with our adjustments. We all listened to what you said in the meeting the other day and came to the conclusion that you could help us resolve this. Would you be willing to?"

"Of course Dom, but I think it's gonna take more than just a few minutes here and there between running the plant."

"Don't worry about that. What I'd like to do is have you form a team. Pick whoever you want to be on it. Say, one person from each functional area, and I'll see that they are reassigned to you one hundred percent. You will report directly to me, and Jim (my own boss) will take over the plant. I want you to debrief Jim after this meeting on everything going on, and assign all your responsibilities and projects to him effective immediately. I'll put something together on the announcement and you can review it and make any changes before we send it out. How about it, will you do it? It would mean a lot to the division if you did."

I looked at the startled look on my boss's face as if he didn't know this was coming and the shock of him having to run the plant. I looked at the General Manager smiling at me waiting for my reply then I spoke.

"Well, I guess that'll work. The team is a great idea because it'll require a cross functional knowledge base. Sure, I'll do it. I know we can fix it."

"Great! Then when you figure out your team let me know. What I'd like you to do is map the entire process of transactions from the start of a product to the finish. Then test each one to make sure that what is supposed to happen does. Report all your findings to me as they occur."

"That sounds like a good plan. I know who I want on the team."

"Great, tell me their names and I'll start on their reassignment." After I told him their names, we ended the meeting and I went into my boss's office. We agreed to meet in a few minutes, after I had listed all the items he would need to take over.

We did so, and the ball was rolling. The only problem was the way the news was received.

The General Manager wrote up an announcement that I read quickly and agreed it said what it needed to. I made no changes and it went out to the division and the plant itself. I had already explained it to my supervisors but the feedback from the floor that they came back with shocked me. Likewise, I received feedback from corporate that showed that they misinterpreted it as well. But the damage was done already.

The memo said that the division was loosing money at an alarming rate and that inventories were having shrinks that couldn't be defined. I was being reassigned and would no longer be Plant Manager but be on special assignment to the General Manager. Well, that sounded okay to me, but what people interpreted it as was that things were messed up and it was my fault so I was reassigned. My supervisors were trying to do damage control on the floor and explain it to people. I was trying to explain the situation to corporate folks as well. But the overall feeling was the same that I screwed up and I was being removed from my position. Yeesh! Now my ego was a wreck and I would carry this label for a long time to come. I guess that was part of the learning and it did turn out to be so. I didn't realize it then that my ego needed to be squished a bit but I did learn it later.

I formed the group and we were very successful. We made headway in the first week. I had a dream at one point seeing programming code and the sequence 060 in the dream. I asked the programmer to check sequence 060 on his programs to see if there was something amiss, as it turned out, that was one of the major problems. All in all we ended up finding 65 different problems that were fixed.

My old boss never did end up running the plant but another former plant manager was assigned to the task. I was asked if I was interested in being part of a Division Manufacturing Services group being formed with a person I respected and liked that would be my boss. I would get a promotion from it as well that included a raise in pay and bonuses. It wasn't an Operations job like a Plant Manager so I wouldn't have the twenty four/seven problem and could spend more time at home. I would make my own schedule basically and all the things I had written on my intention list had come true. I accepted the position. The promotion didn't get announced for a year and thus the ego issues remained for me as well as the others in the newly formed group. But, that was just a way of learning not to worry about what others thought. It was hard, but it was what it was, and I was satisfied for now with such a change, though my ego had to pay the price.

In the new group I had a number of different projects going on and was enjoying my new found freedom at work and time at home. I actually had to figure out what to do on Saturday mornings and I didn't realize how totally absorbed I was in my old job. When I went on vacation with my family I couldn't believe how nice it was not calling into the plant and not thinking about work 24/7. I had found a new me.

Then, one day I was thinking how else I might improve this job, and started to write down my intentions again. One of the things that always bugged me was dressing up for work. It used to be with ties in the old days but now was a thing called work "casual". That was an improvement, but the way I liked to dress the most was in jeans. Nice clean neat jeans. So that was one of the things I wrote down, "Being able to wear jeans to work each day".

Another thing I wanted was more private time at home. Not that I didn't love my family, but with my newfound time available at home I wanted to make more of it for myself, and so, I wrote that down. Well, be careful what you ask for, because you just might get it.

As time moved forward the division decided to take a look at a consulting group involved in taking cost out of organizations. They came in and swept through a plant making changes rapidly and revising the culture of that plant. It was meant to improve profits and improve communications and relationships in the plant. We had a plant within a days drive from us that was in need of such a plan more than any other plant. We had a meeting to review this consultants plan and methods.

The initial meeting was a flop, from what I could tell, and the guy giving it gave me a rotten feeling. Our HR manager asked me on the side about what I thought.

"So A.J., what did you think?"

"I think the guys a creep and I could never trust him. Milt, you know how I am with interviewing people and what I think of them. I can usually tell a person pretty well but I never got such a negative feeling about someone. I don't feel good about this guy!"

"Wow!" He looked at me waiting for some more commentary, as HR people sometimes do, by trying to make me fill the pause in conversation. I looked at him and waited, knowing what he was doing. He started again knowing I wasn't responding to his pause.

"What makes you say that?"

"Just a feeling. But you can also add that he didn't answer the questions very well, and he was cocky as hell, and he thought he was some hot stuff. Then, he asked for the check from Jim in order to start the survey. Thus, he has a cash flow problem. Not my idea of a reputable company to deal with."

"So you wouldn't want to work with him?"

"Milt, what do you think?"

"Okay, I have to tell you I felt uncomfortable with him a bit too."

"Gee, thanks for sharing that."

It wasn't very long that this guy was back in the building. No one knew why. I assumed to get background from others that had worked in the plant he was supposed to fix. He had meetings with me and a few others. The next thing I knew, my boss was asking me if I'd go to that plant and work with this guy. I'd be able to get an apartment so I wouldn't have to stay at hotels and could come back each weekend but it was going to be about a six-month stint. He said he'd understand if I didn't want to, but that it would be an important learning experience for me and would be a great benefit for the division. They needed someone who knew the production control systems, etc and they felt I was the most knowledgeable.

"I'll do it for you and the division, not for that guy." I want to have my role clearly defined with him along with a time frame so this doesn't drag out."

"I think you should. Will you do it?"

"I'll do it. Sadie won't be happy and I won't exactly enjoy this but I'll do it. I wouldn't have done it for other people you know. For you I will, since I trust you."

This thing was a wreck. This guy was totally disorganized which led to a lot of wasted effort. He formed this secret society inside the facility that usurped the plant manager's authority there along with his whole staff. This guy was allowed to reorganize the organization any way he wanted, and if it wasn't done in his time frame, (24 hours after he said it had to happen) he started to charge us more. I got wrapped up in the dynamics of it and was a puppet for this guy. I couldn't believe what I did after reflecting on it after the assignment was over.

The only thing I could think of to violate my initial intuition of not trusting this guy was the power he had over people. It was intriguing to see how he could do anything he pleased. I couldn't figure out how he did it. But then, it struck me when he came into the office we were in and said what a guy on the floor said about him.

A New Reality

"You know what that jerk said about me? He said he wouldn't shake my hand cause I was 'ungodlike.' I told him I was very 'Godlike.'"

I decided to make another appointment with Marilyna to see what turned up.

The Aura Reader - The Second Time

It was an unusually warm winter this year, and this particular December 11, 1999 day followed suit. I was supposed to get the oil changed in the van this morning but my wife had plans to use it to haul our kids and some others to a ceramics class to make some Christmas gifts for the grandparents. So, when I got out of the house at nine in the morning, I got in the car and realized I hadn't anything to do until ten thirty. As I drove off, I thought of different things I could do. I decided to go to Katherine's and get some free coffee with Irish Crème and some cookies before heading out to my ten thirty meeting with Marilyna.

I walked into Katherine's shop, said good morning to everyone and helped myself to some coffee and cookies. I received some inquisitive looks and a strange look of panic from Jo as I went around the corner. Then as I returned with my mug of coffee and sat in the chair she spoke up.

"You don't have an appointment today do you? Kath isn't even in yet."

"No I don't but I had some time to kill and free coffee and cookies sounded good to me. These cookies are a lot better than the ones she puts out when I do have an appointment! What do you do, put stale cookies out for me and put out the good ones after I leave?

I was going to see Marilyna this morning and I ended up having some available time so here I am to brighten your day."

"Well I'm glad to see you made yourself comfortable! No spinning in the chair with the coffee though okay?" Jo stopped eating her breakfast long enough to have that conversation then went back at it.

I sipped my coffee and looked around, Lizzy came over to say hi.

"Who's Marilyna?"

"She's a reader I went to before that Kath recommended. I went to her before and it was pretty interesting. She hit a number of things right on the head."

"I've always wanted to go to one but I don't want to go to a charlatan and have them just take my money, ya know? I am kinda into those things. The book the Celestine Prophecy, did you ever read that?"

"Yeah, I have and the follow up called, The Experiential Guide."

"Yeah I believe in all that and it makes a lot of sense to me. Tell me about the reader. What happened last time that convinced you she was real?"

"A number of things. I have a write up that I made from the notes I took that day and the things that happened after. It's in my car since I was going to give it to Marilyna when I went there today. Want to read it? It's only about 4 pages?"

"Sure!"

them is a female." (I later found out about the reorganization of the Production Control department at the outlying plant I was working at. Ended up 5 men and a woman were reorganized in duties and levels. It was a critical issue. I wasn't asked my opinion until a bit later, not prior to taking action.)

"I see mountains and you going over them. Tahoe... Reddish color hat and scarf. I don't see you in a ski outfit. Red means assertiveness or aggression or anger, aggression being caged in. I feel it has a lot to do with work, are you thinking of changing positions? There is a sideways job that is offered to you. It won't be good to take as it is eliminated after. Out out of the system so stay where you are." (Yes I was offered the Plant Manager job there recently. They tried to talk me into it a few times. I turned it down, as it was a lateral move and I had done that for 9 years already in another plant. We ended up closing the plant so the job was eliminated as she said it would be.)

"I'm going to the woman now."

I got confused at this point and had to ask.

"What woman?"

"The woman at the beginning that you are having trouble communicating with, the one that can be sharp with her tongue the only way she can get what she wants. I feel darkness around her and feel she has a father issue."

"You have a son. Is he fourteen? No he isn't and he isn't your son. I see a 14-year-old and his clothes are older, an older time. He has a gray tee shirt of sorts with a pocket on it and a black line

"Your root chakra looks a little dim. Money problems? No. I think it is attributable to the relationship. I'd like to use the cards now if you don't mind?"

"No problem."

Marilyna took a deck of Tarot cards and shuffled them and spread them out before me. She had me select three then continued.

"A scrap with a young person at work. This new boss is younger than the other boss and about your age group (true). This person, the bosses' result will be unfavorable. Victory is being won in changing the bosses' perception. Someone has been speaking to this younger boss into his ear and misinforming him about you. (True again) You have two bosses. One you get along with well and the other so. This one is more approachable. Your best bet is going through him but staying on your toes. This person is more intimidating and the other wants to please and make everyone happy." (True again.)

I took more cards from time to time as she laid them out on the table and continued reading them. She laughed as she continued on.

"Ha ha ha no pregnancies coming… This is a moving card. Could be looking for a move…. You don't have to stand your ground. You have a good reputation and deal with many people and are very good at it. You are looking for someone to hold your hand but not chain your soul. I feel a walking away. You won't have to guard your principles in any way with work. The girl you have those communication problems with (Sharon) does. She (Sharon) has darker hair than you….not quite as light. The main thing here is she doesn't know what you want. Sometimes it's better to be on your own. I feel a sense of independence. There has been a gradual change in your self and this person has helped you with that but you're not sure where you want to be or go. Sometimes this signifies a new person coming into your life for the better. Let me go to your aura.

"I see blue in it. You were in a long-term relationship. I see a little yellow and pink. You are very giving…an attentive friend and lover. It's not easy for you to receive. The other color I see is lavender. Lavender is spirituality. Saint Germain. Read up on him he will help you."

Aaaaaaaa……..you'd be better at I-Chin than Yoga. The blueness shows you as a very loyal friend and family member. You were raised Catholic and always go above and beyond the call of duty so to speak. You do this in your daily activities. Saying good morning and smiling and treating people nicely. I see you opening a door for someone, yes you are a gentleman."

"I see a lot of white in your aura. Not much fragments. You're balancing energies better now. I see a glitter, which says you're going through this experience you didn't get to do as a child. Enjoy it. I hear music playing and it is very healing for you. You are a dancer?"

"No, I'm not a dancer," I laughed.

"Well I see you dancing by yourself. It is good for you. You, ah, you aren't alone. It connects you with God. You dance alone with God. It is very good for you."

I thought about my "dancing" with my Zen luna sticks outside in the driveway in the summer. It was more exercise than dancing and I did it to music but I guess that could be considered dancing. I'd do it almost an hour every night and it was very connecting for me. I can believe she saw me dancing by myself.

"The car. With your car. The tires….one in the back on the passenger side and the other…have you checked them? Check the tires. Do you change cars? I see a white one. I feel good with the car you have. Keep it and carry a fix a flat, or keep a cell phone. I would check out the tires. It's due for a tune up. The wipers are okay."

"I feel someone from the other side. Someone who drank only tea (Beth only drinks tea)….an older woman with money that was very frugal. She is named Sarah. I will ask her to move on. She is showing me a broken old-fashioned mirror. Sarah was quite a looker too! The mirror, the brush, the comb are from another time. She is sitting in front of a vanity. Some things she would splurge on were silk and nightgowns and a well made bed. 1800's with her. End of 1800's and maybe early 1900's, tea balls… Had a nice flat not a home. A unique terrace with a garden area…nice…. Male gentleman and a small child, a female, next to her, her name is Liddia. The gentleman isn't giving his name, oh yes, he is Mr. Death. These two perished together in a fire. Something was knocked over and I see fire. The two died together. Why is that scene there? I don't know how it applies to you."

"The next scene is a man and a woman in the Victorian era. I see a pendant being passed to her from another. You were very happy....a middle income male at this point. Nice celebration. I see a sideshow, or entertainment, on the grounds. You row to the landing and walk with her to the show. Magic show, very nice union, you've been looking for her since. A very strong kindred spirit or soul mate, she is, I think, in California now. Your hair was much darker and you were taller then with Sarah. You have the same eyes now, same eyes.

"In this lifetime, you have always been in your line of work in other lifetimes. But for this lifetime you are really learning to balance your female and male energies. You're doing well with that very well. It's important you've come to this balancing. You're very busy but you should get into something soul developing. There is a spark of enlightenment for you in the book, 'The Vision.' Your time in the car is church for you, it's good. You needed to be there now. You get messages doing that. (True again. I had just been listening to the audio tapes of "The Vision" in the car and found some useful information in them.)

I checked my tires and got a cell phone for the car for traveling and put a fix a flat can in both the car and the van. The tires on the car seemed fine but I did need to repair the anti lock brake system on the driver side rear wheel since it ended up locking up on me a few days later.

That was about all Marilyna had until we went to the door. She said St. Francis was also watching over me now and there was a female guide that would be with me for the next two to three months as long as I could maintain the feminine energy well enough.

It seems she hit on a few things again but didn't fill me in on that consultant as much as I had hoped for. Maybe now wasn't the time for it. I continued my temporary assignment going between my family and my apartment for the next few months.

More Information Arrives

*"The intellect has little to do on the road to
discovery. There comes a leap in consciousness, call
it intuition or what you will, the solution comes to
you and you don't know how or why."*
-Albert Einstein-

Some time after I had finished the assignment away from home, I had a feeling there was something I needed to know but I didn't know what. I had been to the area book stores over the past few days but nothing jumped out at me, yet I knew there was something I needed to find. Then I went through my books and found the one I had gotten at a book signing. The one with the picture of myself and the author that the author wrote in, "Listen to no one, courage!" I remembered waiting in line at that book store for 4 hours for that signing and just then I felt a rush of energy. Yes, this must mean that I had to go to that very same store. The book I needed right now was there.

I checked to see if the rest of the family wanted to go. It was a week night and about 6:30PM already.

"Anyone want to go to a bookstore?"

"Papa, we've been to all the bookstores in the area already and we have enough books," my son said.

"You can always get another book. I'll buy you guys another book if you want to go. I'll always buy you a book. This store is further away. It has the one I've been looking for."

"What one is that?" Sadie asked.

"I don't know but it's there and we have to go there tonight or it will be gone."

"Okay!" Kara answered without hesitation.

"Let me get my sneaks on!" Sadie called out and we were off.

When we got there I remembered the day of a book signing I had been to at this store. How I bought a hot dog from the entrepreneur who saw the line of people outside and knew how to capitalize on it. We entered the store. It was an old theater that was turned into a bookstore with high ceilings with elaborate crown moldings around the edges. The floor turned into a soft silent carpet and the smell of books filled my nostrils. A smell I remember back to the library in my childhood.

"Can I go look at my section?" Kara asked while Adam looked at me for the answer.

"Yeah go ahead with Mom and I'll be wandering around," I said as Sadie caught up with us.

I started to wander, mentally asking to find this book and still not knowing where, or what, to look for. I wandered all the aisles starting from the back of the store. As I approached the front I could feel a tingle begin to run up from my feet. I knew I was approaching it. I passed one section on an aisle and the feeling grew stronger then faded as I passed it. I backed up. It grew stronger again but it wasn't in this aisle it was in the next one over. I continued to mentally ask for it to show itself and went to the next aisle. The feeling was very strong now and I started to scan the cases with my hand. As I approached a book, it practically zapped me.

I couldn't read the title on the binding as it was upside down. It was the only one of its kind on the shelf. I pulled it out and as I flipped the cover and read the inscription from the author which said, "Blessings" followed by the authors signature in an unrecognizable scroll. The title was "Book of Shadows." A mystery I thought? It sounded like an old series that was on TV when I was a kid. I flipped the pages open. I read a sentence in the lower portion of the page that said, "I read that physicists had discovered a new level of reality. Underlying the three dimensional physical world described by Newton's laws, they found an invisible realm, a quantum level of subatomic particles and energy."

I looked at the part about the author. She was a lawyer that had a strange series of coincidences that led her to become a Wiccan priestess. This book was about a real witch and she was talking about the things I had been thinking about. Physics and witchcraft? Hmm, I had to buy the book. This was why I came here. The electricity running through me subsided now and a feeling of cool and calm filled me as I flipped the book shut and went to find the rest of the family. They selected some books and we took them to the counter. The woman at the register began to ring them up. She got to mine.

"You're lucky you got this one. We had a signing from the author this week and she signed the ones that remained. We had a few this morning. We'd probably not have this one tomorrow. She was a really nice author, some of them aren't so nice, ya know?"

"Like everyone I guess."

"I guess but they are such public figures and their fans are here so you'd think they'd be nicer to them, like this author was. Anyway, I think you got a prize today with this one."

"Thanks, I guess I have."

We went home and I dove into the book. Let me tell you a bit more about it first.

The author, Phyllis Curott, *JD, (For those that didn't know, JD means she is a lawyer, Jurum Doctor)(Book of Shadows, Broadway Books, NY, 1998)* has been on several television interviews and has addressed the public, church congregations, the media, the legal system, The Parliament of the World's Religions and United Nations conferences. Her book is written in a fictional style though it is a true story. She had a series of mysterious coincidences that led her to this world of Wicca and, as she says in the introduction, "I entered a realm of magic that was as ancient as the history of humanity, and as modern as the theories of quantum physics."

Phyllis was schooled as a lawyer from New York University law school. She used her doctorate as a high powered counselor in a prestigious law firm to practice law for the Rock Stars before she became a High Priestess. As she says in her book about her experience, "Aldous Huxley referred to these experiences as an 'opening of the doors of perception.'"

As it turned out, this book had a lot of similarities to my own story. I didn't end up becoming a Wiccan Priestess but I did open my eyes to another piece of interrelated information about this new world that as constantly looming up before me. She had some similar experiences to mine as well. This book also had the effect of teaching me a bit about what a witch was, and it **wasn't** what I had been told, or what the general perception of what witchcraft was. I ended up learning more about it and even became good friends with a witch that was a very wonderful person. More about her later.

One of the things Dr. Curott mentioned was how she felt like she was loosing her grip. Her "logical, rational self" didn't approve of the extrasensory occurrences that were happening to her, much the same as I didn't. She, as a lawyer, was trained in logic and rational thinking as I, an engineer, was. That is, to be logical and rational and pay strict attention to the facts, and the facts alone. There wasn't any room in our minds for the paranormal things that had occurred to us.

Dr. Curott spoke of her occurrences starting in 1978 and said that time period matched up with a certain astrological occurrence that happened every twenty years or so. Well, my world changed at the end of 1997 into 1998. That was when all the strange things started to happen to me, twenty years after 1978. Then they subsided, and only happened randomly or when I opened for them to.

This time period that happened every twenty years or so was supposed to be a time during which doorways to previously unperceived realities were opened. Dr. Currot said she was, "…experiencing a shamanic break, a break with the socially defined reality opening to a greater reality of a sacred, living universe. Some Native Americans, and Witches, would describe it as 'a calling.' Aldous Huxley referred to these experiences as an opening of the doors of perception……." (page 8).

She continued.

"…At the quantum level everything is interconnected energy, even matter. Quantum reality is another level of existence, another dimension. Here the energy field is the underlying order, a hidden, or shadow, reality of our daily lives. We see solid material objects as separated from one another - a rock, a table, a human being-but on the quantum level, they are all actually bundles of vibrating interacting energy. As Einstein said, 'Our separation from each other is an optical illusion of consciousness.'"

It seemed to me that this woman was **very much** like me in the way things came about and the way she analyzed them to be. She couldn't even see how, when she met her first witch, someone as **smart** as that person could be involved in something **so weird**. She ended up having many of the same life changing experiences that I did in experiencing energy flow, seeing auras and knowing things. She even ended up getting a message about the God Odin as I did. Her message came in a different way than mine but was the same message none the less.

My message came from my friend Zeek. He told me about a weird dream he had one night. He saw me with one eye missing standing split into two full, but connected, forms. One form of me seemed to be disappearing, and my other form was filling with light and energy. The light and energy form was the one with only one eye. Zeek never heard of the person this dream related to, and neither had I, until I came across the information in Dr. Curott's book.

When I read Phyllis's book, and found her passage on Odin, I recognized what that dream had meant for me. As she writes of the tale of Odin she says on page 17, "Odin suffered for nine days, hanging upside down from the Yggdrasil tree, helpless and alone, until a raven plucked an eye from his head. He lost the ability to see, 'normally.' In exchange for his sacrifice, Odin was given the runes, the first letters of a sacred alphabet, which enabled him to see within, to see into the past, into the future, to win the power of wisdom and the gift of inner sight, Odin had to be willing to sacrifice the way in which he had always seen the world." It seemed to me that was exactly what was happening to both of us. The world would never look the same.

Dr. Currot spoke of how the persecutions ran the witches out and how the churches had to eliminate these powerful women in order to create the patriarchal religions, so males could have power and control of the masses. The Vatican edict from the late 1400's issued by Pope Innocent VIII stated witches worshipped Satan and to this day has never been rescinded. That's ironic since witches don't even believe in a Satan. Again, news to me. The more I researched it, the more I found that this was so. I'll go into Wicca or, known by the old name, of witchcraft, a bit more here.

A New Reality

Wicca is an earth based "religion," if you will, though it carries none of the controlling aspects of organized religions. Though a close look at what the priest in the Catholic religion does during services will reveal a startling similarity in rituals. Robes and symbols, candles and altars, layouts of churches, etc. All have their roots in the early beliefs that formed from Egypt and possibly before.

There is startling similarity in Wicca to Shamanism as well. Shamans and Wiccans, though seemingly from different origins, have similar ways in their beliefs and rituals. Shamanism was a part of the American Indians, as well as the South American Indians. Though again, they differ some yet they have much similarity. The Toltecs were Shamanistic.

Merlin of King Arthur fame falls into this category of Wiccan in a way as well. He was called a Wizard or a Magician. This area of the mysteries is called Magick with a "k" and people who practice it are sometimes referred to as a Sorcerer, though that term is also sometimes used to describe a South American Naugal Shaman.

The Wiccans I have met have all been very considerate of others and their beliefs as well as open minded and loving of others, which is a far cry from the standard organized religion induced view, or society's commonly held perception of them. When one considers the history of the organized, patriarchal, religions and the purpose of controlling the populace being one of paramount importance in those times of Lords and Ladies, one can see why it was necessary to get rid of the witches to be able to have control.

The golden rule in Wicca is, "HARM YE NONE, DO WHAT THOU WILL." This applies in all situations including harming ones feelings, emotions or, physical harm. In other words, do whatever you want, but don't harm anyone, in any way, by doing it. All people should live to such a wonderful simple rule. Makes it pretty easy to determine whether to do something or not, doesn't it?

Let's see. I have to decide whether or not to cheat on my wife. Hmm. Will it cause her harm if I did? Probably. Then the answer is don't do it. Easy isn't it?

How about another example. Should I steal? Answer, it is detrimental to the other person so no. Should I tell them what a jerk they are? Answer, no, because that would hurt their feelings. Should I treat anyone differently regardless of their race, or gender, or sexual preference? Of course not, that would be harmful to them in their feelings about themselves and their rights as human beings. Beats the hell out of trying to vote on the some 1800 rules that a largely popular organized religion were recently doing in a 2 week long council meeting to make more rules for their brethren doesn't it? But, then again, I may not be as smart as them because I don't think I'd remember them all.

Have you ever heard of Free Masonry? It is a society that has a pledge of death upon entering if the secrets are discussed with anyone who isn't a Free Mason. In the time that this was instituted this was certainly a necessary rule to preserve the order from death itself. Thus, unless you are one, it is unlikely that you know much about it, though there are some books about it out there. Its roots were pre-Christian and have similar ritual to Wicca and to others that use the Kaballah (otherwise known as the "Tree of Life," which is included in both Christian and Jewish Mystics study). Free Masonry believes in learning and helping others and is a very forthright society. Some of its spirituality was lost in some cases and became a social club more than a way to learn the mysteries. Nonetheless, it does have many of the same roots as Wicca in ritual and beliefs and there were many of our founding fathers that were a part of them. As a matter of fact all of the signers of the Constitution of the United States were official Free Masons except for two that have some question as to whether they were or not. If you were to investigate it you would find the similarities in Free Masonry to Wicca.

So what is Wicca really?

Simply stated, Wicca is witchcraft. There are many forms of Wicca. Due to their belief in Karma, in true witchcraft there is very little room for what is commonly called black magic. Black magic is generally thought of to be practiced by anyone who is a witch but that is far from true. The "Harm ye none" rule was a warning to prevent black magic. That rule, along with their belief in Karma that any harm done to anyone will return to the doer three times as great, diminishes the black magic as a very active part of it. I will quote the work of a foremost authority in this field who recently passed on. He and his wife wrote the book. The title is, "The Witches Way, Principles, Rituals and Beliefs of Modern Witchcraft" by Janet and Stewart Farrar. Their words are below:

"Witches are neither fools, escapists nor superstitious. They are living in the twentieth century, not in the middle ages, and they accept the fact without reservation; if they do tend to have a keener sense of historical continuity, and a broader time canvas, than most people, that makes their awareness of the present more vivid, not less. Many witches are scientists or technicians, and in our experience, often very good ones. If modern witchcraft did not have a coherent rationale, such people could only keep going by a kind of deliberate schizophrenia, with neither watertight compartment of their lives particularly happy - and we have seen no signs of that.

"Modern witchcraft does have a rationale and a very coherent one. This may surprise some of our readers, who know only that witchcraft comes from the gut. And so it does, as far as motivation and operation go. The working power and the appeal of the craft do arise from the emotions, the intuition, the 'vasty deep' of the Collective Unconscious. Its Gods and Goddesses draw forms from the numinous Archetypes which are the mighty foundation stones of the human racial psyche (I believe this was meant to be "rational" not racial).

"The rationale of Wicca is a philosophical framework into which every phenomenon, from chemistry to clairvoyance, from logarithms to love, can be reasonably fitted. The rationale of Wicca rests on two fundamental principles: The Theory of Levels and the Theory of Polarity.

A New Reality

"The Theory of Levels maintains that reality exists and operates on many planes (or I might note "dimensions" versus levels, as the Quantum Physicists have found).

"The Theory of Polarity maintains that all activity, all manifestations, arise from (and it is inconceivable without) the interaction of pairs and complimentary opposites, this polarity is not a conflict between good and evil but a creative tension like that between the terminals of a battery." Sounds a little like an atom again doesn't it? Electrons and Protons, negative and positive.

They continue.

"If one pushes the investigation of the physical plane to its utmost frontiers, the very nature of those frontiers brings one face to face with the areas of interaction with other planes; one keeps getting puzzling glimpses over the boundary wall - and it becomes increasingly difficult to ignore what lies beyond.

"Witches are practical people; philosophy to them is not just an intellectual exercise - they have to put it into practice in their everyday lives, and in their working, if philosophy is to have any meaning. Similarly, much as they trust instinct, they do not merely blunder ahead in response to its promptings without any reference to logic - they prefer to understand what they are doing, and why."

On page 140 a bit more and then that's all from them for now.

"It would be a waste of words, here, to reiterate the "normal" basic ethical codes which are common to every *decent* Christian, Jew, Moslem, Hindu, Buddhist, Pagan, Atheist or what have you -

the rules of respect for one's neighbor, of civic responsibility, of parental care, of truthfulness and honesty, of concern for the underprivileged, and so on. These are fundamental human standards which the vast majority acknowledge and try with varying success to live up to. It goes without saying that witches do the same.

"What we are concerned with here are the rules of conduct which are special to witches, or on which they lay their special emphasis, because of the nature of the philosophy and their activities.

"Perhaps the most important of these special areas is magic.

"If you deliberately set out to develop your psychic abilities you are awakening a faculty by which you can influence other people, with or without their knowledge; a faculty by which you can obtain information in ways that they do not expect or allow for; a faculty by which you can either enhance their life energy or sap it. By which you can help or harm them.

"Obviously you are taking a great responsibility on yourself and this calls for a set of willingly accepted rules. And these rules are all the more important because very often only you know if you are honestly obeying them. The observance or non-observance of these rules is precisely what distinguishes 'white' from 'black' working."

Now you say ahhhh there is more than one rule! He just contradicted himself! Ha! Well wait and see as they continue.

"All these rules are summed up in the phrase, 'And it harm none.' A witch must never use his or her powers in a way which will cause harm to anyone -or even frighten anyone by claiming to.

Another Wiccan rule says: Never boast, never threaten, never say you would wish ill of anyone."

Of course that is summed up in the first no harm rule when one realizes that a witches intentions can cause harm or good.

Thus, it seems that what I had previously thought was the truth about witches was nothing more than an Easter bunny tale made up of similar falsehoods. In fact, it seems that witches and wizards and sorcerers are much closer in nature to our present, more accepted, explorers of the unseen realms called Physicists.

How can I find one of these beings? Find a witch, or shaman, or wizard, per se? Would they really be as the book said or would they be some uneducated junkie dealing with half a deck and a bunch of delusions operating in an anti-social, radicalist, "in your face" way? How could I be so lucky to find them now that I know what they really were?

Maybe it won't be luck. Maybe I'm somehow meant to meet them to learn more and continue on my journey. Maybe I'm not *meant* to do anything but the fact that I have the intention and desire to meet one, maybe I will somehow meet them through a quantum exchange of sorts. I did long for some new and different friends to break outside my perception of what the world is from my limited manufacturing perspective. Yes I'd like to meet one of these hidden, secret ones. Well, the intention was set. Little did I know how well the intention would operate.

Arrival at the Plateau

There was something strange about this consultant, my second boss, that I couldn't place for a while. I had overridden my instincts on him and had accepted him. The one that I vehemently said I would never trust when he gave his presentation to us at the onset was now someone I trusted?

One day, after my assignment away from home and after I had learned about witches, I had a revelation. I figured out why we were puppets for this guy and why he used the symbology in his literature and advertising as he did. Why did he have the number of steps in his process that he did and why did the acronym for his process match the name of a Goddess of the Bask Pantheon? Not to mention the raising of energy in his meetings with his forced group physical activity preceding his meetings. Why did he say he was "Very Godlike!!" when someone claimed he was "ungodlike." Why did he comment on me not having any fear and so much energy? How did he manipulate the group into the puppets we turned into for him? Well, I was glad I had ended the assignment when I did.

I was able to get back to my office again and started on the other things I was doing before I left. I read the second note I made for what I wanted out of life and work. I was stunned. I found out I had gotten what I asked for again. Wear jeans to work everyday. I did down there as it was normal attire. Private time for myself. I had lots when I was stuck in that apartment every night with no family! Be excited about my work. I was very excited for a time there before I realized what had happened. 12 and 14-hour days were normal. I had been taken and used as a pawn though I had gotten everything I had "intended" on my list. Be *careful* what you wish for as the old saying was now proven to be true.

I looked up his web site and sent some of the information around our business that was false on it and then went into the same shared drives he used on our system and started to look at what was happening lately. I ended up getting locked out of the shared drive. I could hear him telling them to take away my security. He used to tell me I couldn't even tell my real boss what was going on. When he caught me talking to my real boss on the phone he'd give me hell after. Now he locked me out of the shared drive.

Then one night I was sitting on the recliner at home and felt like someone connected to me. It was as if I had connected to Beth but I knew it wasn't her. It was a very draining feeling. Then I could feel a palpitation in my chest. It scared me enough that I almost went to the emergency room. I concentrated on making it go away, tried to shield myself and I had success at that, or it just subsided.

When I went to lunch the next day my friend told me of the scare he had last night. He described what had happened to me exactly. It was as if it happened to both of us. I told him what happened to me and we compared notes. The time was the same when it happened as well. I thought now that I had felt it happen to him. That maybe he did have a heart problem and I felt it.

The next night it happened again, not as bad but when I went to bed that night another strange thing occurred. Our dog started growling as if someone else was in the room. We had been sleeping and then the bed shook as if there was an earthquake or something. The dog growled fiercely and I felt as if there was someone else in the room. She is normally very quiet at night. Something was frightening her.

I could see in the room well enough by the light coming through the window and there was no one there. There seemed to be a presence of something but no one physically there. I thought in a scream in my head, "Get out of here or I will certainly track you down and destroy you!"

Had this been a psychic attack of some sort? Had that been what was happening to me the past nights with the energy draining me and the palpitations in my chest? Maybe. My friend Zeek and I discussed it the next day. We agreed to mentally shield ourselves that night and to will the intruder to have any damage done to us return back to him instead and to bind him in causing any other harm. That day at work I also took all the files from that project and the book this person wrote and bound it all up in tape. I passed the intention that he should gain no further work with our division and stay away from us. Whether it was a game in our minds, or not, it worked.

Neither Zeek nor I had any further problems. In addition, the division stopped using him for any further projects. The corporation no longer recommended him for any work. As an added coincidence a pain I got in my left neck when I was on that assignment just disappeared and never returned. I noticed it when I went to sleep that night. Had that been the connection he had on me somehow? He used to ask me about it all the time and compare how his felt. He would put his hand on my shoulder there to squeeze it. He acted as if he had the same ailment. In any case, the things Zeek and I did, games of the mind or not, worked and took away another problem with it, my neck pain.

It was during this assignment that my wife found an article in the local paper about a woman who had a shop in a quaint old town in Ohio. She organized drum circles and sold drums from her store, neither of which I had any interest in at the time. But Sadie cut it out of the paper and saved it for me. The part that was interesting was she had a metaphysical gift store in a small town not far from us. But more interesting was what I felt when I looked upon her picture. She was sitting on the floor posing as if playing a hand drum and smiling. She had a look to her and feeling about her that I sensed this would be a new friend. It felt as if I already knew her somehow though her features weren't the least bit familiar.

I went to her store the following Saturday but she wasn't there. Someone else was working. They did say she'd be there next Saturday though. I checked the time the store opened on the door on the way out and decided to come back the next weekend.

The following Saturday morning I went down to her store. First I went to the corner deli and bought some pumpkin roll and a couple of coffees. Then I went to her shop and sat outside on the bench. It was supposed to open at ten thirty. I sat on the bench and smoked a cigarette and enjoyed the sunny, warm, fall day it was. It was about ten of eleven when I had noticed she had unlocked the door.

I walked into the entryway smelling the fragrant gentleness of the incense that was, evidently, burned regularly. I passed the waterfall, with its surrounding statues of Goddesses and the floral and vine decorations, and into the store itself. It overwhelmed me how well decorated it was and how much there was to look at. I wandered about looking at things and thought, a witch owned this store. She was a witch. I was glad I knew what a witch really was now and not what I had been taught as a child.

I had been having discussions with my wife about not having many people that I could talk to about the strange things that went on in my life and how nice it would be to have someone close by that could relate to me. Pink monkeys needed friends too! I knew this person would be that for me. She entered the shop from the backroom.

"Hey there!" She beamed out in a cheerful, happy greeting.

"Hey there!"

"Can I help you?"

"Oh just looking around a bit. You've got a nice shop here."

"Why, thanks for saying so."

"How long have you been here?"

"I think it's about six months now."

"No wonder I hadn't seen it before. My wife saw your article in the paper with your picture and showed it to me. That's how I found out about it. It seems the timing was good as well."

"The timing?"

"Yeah, the timing. You see, there have been a lot of strange things going on with my life lately and there aren't many people around that wouldn't think I was crazy if I talked to them about it. I knew when I saw your picture that you were someone who wouldn't think I was nuts."

"Oh yeah? What makes you say that?"

"Well you have a 'metaphysical' store. That says a lot right there. But mostly just looking at you I feel you are going to be a good friend."

"Ha ha ha. Don't you think that's a bit presumptuous?"

"Not really. You can tell those things at times I'm sure. This is that way."

She smiled as she looked at me and I stood there grinning.

I put the coffees and the bag of pumpkin rolls on the counter.

"I hope you don't mind, I bought a couple of coffees and some pumpkin rolls, 'presumptuously' thinking you would share them with me…if you're interested."

"Well! Sure. That sounds wonderful! You've got my attention now. So what kind of strange things have been happening?"

I started by telling her the story about meeting Beth and some of the things that happened along the way. She listened intently as we ate and drank and then she responded.

"You're not nuts. You're just opening up and experiencing what's always been there. Things like that happen to people."

"Have you had things like that happen?"

"Well I can't say that the exact things have happened to me, but I can say that I have learned there is much more to life than most people give it credit for. Most people just live their lives on the surface, never really experiencing all the fullness and complexity there is. They are never able to break free from the bindings the lives they are involved in create for them. I like to call them, 'surface dwellers.'"

"So tell me more about yourself, where you came from, and how you got here."

"Well let's see. I'm Portuguese and was raised in Canada. I lived there, teaching English as a second language…"

We talked and talked until it was time for me to leave. When it was, I asked if it would be okay for me to come back next Saturday, and would she like the same coffee and pumpkin roll. Asha did, and I left feeling I had just been given a gift. I'd been given the gift of a new friend to work through the incidents and things that I could never have worked through with anyone else around me. Over time she determined we were probably kindred spirits of some sort. She helped me immeasurably as the months and years passed.

It wasn't a long time until I had the dream about the Plateau again. It reran like an old movie in my head. I saw a tall rock plateau that was too slippery to climb or drive up. I tried to climb on the roof of an adjoining house to get to the plateau but kept falling through the roof while my wife stood beside me and didn't leave me. When I got back out of the house and looked up at the plateau the rain had stopped and the rocks were dry. The person waiting for me from before was there. I could tell who it was now. It was my new friend, Asha, the one on the plateau. She was there for me when I reached the plateau.

I guess the rain had stopped and I now had reached the plateau. There wasn't the miserable struggling that my job used to be. It was peaceful and I was able to set my own schedule. Yes, the rain had stopped so I was now at a plateau. A place of relative rest and, my friend Asha was here to help me on this level. How long would I be on this plateau I wasn't sure, but it was better to be here than where I was before.

Yes the rain had stopped. For the kids' sake, we wanted to stay in the neighborhood if we moved. It was a great neighborhood with great schools. We had a few houses sell in the area and we were originally thinking we might skip moving into a bigger house and just get the one we were in paid off. Then, one day my wife went for a walk and when she came back, she said,

"It's a good thing DeeDee is buying the house down the street because if she wasn't it would be perfect for us."

"What house down the street?"

"The one down on the second cul-de-sac from the top..."

She described it to me. I could tell from the way she spoke that this was going to be our house.

"DeeDee's not going to buy it."

"Yes she is! She's going to put a bid in on it. She was there and she told me she was."

"She's not going to buy it, we are."

"What!?"

"Yup, mark my words. You'll see. I can tell just the way you're talking about it."

I was out of town the following week, and when I called, my daughter told me that Dee Dee wasn't going to buy it. I told Sadie to put in a bid but she refused to. When I got back, we went to an open house that Friday and we put in a bid, and put our house up for sale with the same realtor contingent on the acceptance. The deal flew through the process and we had our house sold in three weeks and we were in the new one. And that was at the time of year that wasn't always good to sell. It was late October and schools were in session and people didn't move much at that time, but it all worked out, and we had money to spare to furnish the new one. Since it was twice the size of the old one we needed to buy a lot of things to fill it, but it all worked out, perfectly.

So now it happened. Our lives were getting better still and things were happening like in a dream. I never would have thought that things could get better by letting go of control versus being controlling, yet they had. I had gone through the most out of control portion of my life and had actually helped by figuratively, "throwing the oars out of the boat" like I had thought of in the driveway when trying to decide what to do about my job. Letting go of control brought me to here from there. A better place to be.

There is now more love in my life, and more living being done, but I can tell, and KNOW, that this is just the beginning and not the end of it. That there is so much more to learn and to expand into yet. I've had to question any previously held beliefs, and I am still not quite sure how to explain it all, since it all seems to fall into the somewhat unexplainable but possible category.

But, though unexplainable, I have learned to trust in the process. Be it Beth's miracle with her MS, or be it the smaller, but no less important miracles of finding the information to help to keep going on this path, or finding the friends to sustain me. The magic of finding Brad, Beth, Sharon, and Asha at the time I needed them most. Trust in feeling these strange energies, and knowing the messages now as they show up, and being able to believe them. Trust in connecting to others in the most literal sense, though in the most unbelievable manner. Trust in the information obtained in the strangest manners which I should never have been able to know. Trust that we have the ability to have our intentions connect up with reality through synchronicity.

All these things fall out of the realm of the probable but they all, like any event, have the possibility of occurrence. Just like a curve of probabilities, the ones at the outside don't happen often, but they all can happen. That is what has happened. Those are what I call life's miracles.

What were the causes of these things? An overactive imagination? A psychological defect? Whatever unseen forces may have been at work, or whatever caused these things, I am thankful for it as I have been given new eyes to view with, and a new mind to react to this much more amazing world.

 I've learned many things along this path. One of which is it is much more difficult to write a book than it is to write a journal. 7 years have now transpired since I began this process of communicating some of my story to you. However, I did get to create a script in the process as well, though that took some learning to be able to do. It was more fun to do than writing the book was, since I was able to make it more interesting as it is only "based" on the true story that this book is true to.

I learned that what we are taught is not always the way things are, that we form paradigms that we try to fit things into to explain our worlds, and those paradigms are not always correct. We need to break these paradigms in order to see the truth around us.

I learned that love is more important than anything else in this world and truth is more valuable than any perception, truth to one's self and truth to those around you. Where there is truth there is no fear. Where there is love, there is no fear.

I learned that not everything you believe is worth believing, and the things you don't currently believe may well be the most important things to believe.

Beth is still doing fine should you ask. Asha is seen regularly. Sharon, I lost track of in Germany somewhere and Brad was teaching at an alternative school but moved on to another school since and we stay in touch on occasion as he does his catalyst thing.

I hope you have enjoyed my story. I hope it may have helped you in some way in your story. Try not to show being too pink a monkey and find others like yourself. Or at least, let them find you.

Live life to love and learn. If you'd like more detail on how these things can happen read the appendix for a start.

Sincerely,

A.J.

Appendix

<u>The Physics of Consciousness</u>

The title of this addendum is the same as the book I am going to try to summarize for you ("<u>The Physics of Consciousness</u>", Evan Harris Walker, Cambridge Massachusetts, Perseus Books, 2000). Hopefully, I have accurately captured the essence of it here so you might decide if this may in fact be something that is real. I have come to that conclusion, and this book sheds a new light on something previously non scientific.

Let me start with a bit about the author. His name is, Evan Harris Walker. He is the founder and director of the Walker Cancer Institute. He has made major scientific contributions in astronomy, physics, neurophysiology, astrophysics, psychology and medicine. He has a Ph.D. in physics and has published more than a hundred papers in scientific journals and popular magazines and holds a dozen patents. He is intimately familiar with the workings of our brain and mind and the physics that support it. He takes us from Newton to present day in the book and reveals his theory of how consciousness exists and how our will, or intentions, can affect everyday life through Quantum interactions with our surroundings. A true thinker, and great mind of today, and on top of it he writes most eloquently.

A New Reality

In order to reveal what is revealed in the book I will jump in leaps from one concept to the next, trying to connect them to reveal what the book reveals. The book itself does it much better than I, but naturally, I can't insert the whole book here, but give you a taste that then, you may want to read it yourself. The result I want to show is that there is a connection that occurs daily that most of us never know is there, yet, it is a part and parcel of our living in this life.

Where I have put multiple punctuation such as, "..." is where I have skipped over other material to grab the essence only. I start on page seven of the book where the author writes,

"It is easy to imagine fantasy as physical and myth as real. We do it almost every moment. We do this as we dream, as we think, and as we cope with the world about us...In order to put meaning back into our lives, we should recognize illusions for what they are, and we should reach out and touch the fabric of reality...Science has entirely overturned what we know about the structure of the world. But rather than revising our picture of what reality is, we cling to a collage of incongruent shards. We preserve a false assemblage of images, one pasted upon another, so that we can keep unchanged the mental portrait of ourselves and of the world to which we are accustomed. We go about our business despite the fact that the world on which we base our lives is so much in question, so much a mystery...Some loose themselves in doing their jobs at work and cutting the grass at home. They close their eyes to a billion years that have passed and a billion parsecs to the edge of the universe. Reality for them is the fantasy of here and the illusion of now...Others lose themselves in illusions and diversions that are just as far from reality…things that let us live our lives without asking too many questions."

On page 13 the author refers to Harvey Cox another author that wrote, "The Seduction of the Spirit."

Harvey Cox writes, "The truth does exist, and when the truth is honestly sought, with a mind that is ready to accept the truth, whatever the truth turns out to be, then the answers do come, and the answers change people."

This is really the challenge we all have. We have to open our minds to things that seem to be not possible or not acceptable based on our current knowledge and beliefs. We need to be able to cast aside the previous systems or beliefs in order to accept the truth and see the truth. If we can't gain a perspective that is free from prejudice about ideas and concepts foreign to us, we will never really know the truth but some muddy semblance that keeps us self satisfied in our island of ignorance, oblivious to true reality.

Well, what is this strange thing called quantum physics that I am supposed to overturn all my beliefs for in order to gain the truth? What is this mumble jumble other than a thing that a bunch of intellectuals use to toss seemingly imaginary, unintelligible arguments that make no sense to anyone but them, back and forth? Why should this thing that is just an intellectual thing be something that should change my life?

A New Reality

Well quantum physics isn't just intellectual mumble jumble. It has been used for a number of things we are already familiar with. On page 68 of Evan's book he tells about it.

"Quantum mechanics is being used to design new drugs to heal and medicate our bodies. It is being used to understand the delicate machinery of life, of reproduction, of evolution. Its offspring fills our newspapers with tales of nuclear power, worries of nuclear war, designs of weapons for future wars, and defenses for future peace. Its products, such as magnetic resonance imaging (MRI) and positron emission tomography (PET) scans, let us peek into the structural and chemical make-up of the living tissues of the body, and with the aid of the scanning tunneling microscope (STM), we can see individual atoms. The consequences of quantum mechanics- the fruits, the benefits, and the liabilities- permeate our lives. The results are all around us."

There are a number of oddities in the quantum mechanical world that don't seem possible but are. They are very real and have been proven to occur time and time again. One of those oddities is quantum tunneling and it is a thing that goes on inside of our brain to relay our thoughts and feelings and our perceptions of reality. Brian Greene wrote a fun story about quantum tunneling and I will use that to explain what this quantum tunneling is. Starting on page 85 of his book, The Elegant Universe, (New York and London W.W.Norton Co.1999). Brian Greene, a Rhodes scholar and Ph.D. in Physics from Oxford University, writes:

"A bit worn from their trans-solar-system expedition, George and Gracie return to earth and head over to the H-Bar for some post-space-sojourning refreshments. George orders the usual-papaya juice on the rocks for himself and a vodka tonic for Gracie-and kicks back in his chair, hands clasped behind his head, to enjoy a freshly lit cigar. Just as he prepares to inhale, though, he is stunned to find that the cigar must somehow have slipped from between his teeth. Thinking that the cigar must somehow have slipped from his mouth, George sits forward expecting to find it burning a hole in his shirt or trousers. But it is not there. The cigar is not to be found. Gracie, roused by George's frantic movement, glances over and spots the cigar lying on the counter directly *behind* George's chair.

"Strange," George says, "how in the heck could it have fallen over there? It's as if it went right through my head-but my tongue isn't burned and I don't seem to have any new holes." Gracie examines George and reluctantly confirms that his tongue and head appear to be perfectly normal. As the drinks have just arrived, George and Gracie shrug their shoulders and chalk up the fallen cigar to one of life's little mysteries. But the weirdness at the H-Bar continues.

"George looks into his papaya juice and notices that the ice cubes are incessantly rattling around - bouncing off each other and the sides of the glass like overcharged automobiles in a bumper-car arena, and this time he is not alone. Gracie holds up her glass, which is about half the size of George's and both of them see that her ice cubes are bouncing around even more frantically. They can hardly make out the individual cubes as they all blur together into an icy mass. As George and Gracie stare at her rattling drink with wide eyed wonderment, they see a single ice cube pass right *through* the side of her glass and drop down to the bar. They grab the glass and see that it is fully intact; somehow the ice cube went right through the solid glass without causing any damage. "Must be post-space-walk hallucinations," says George. They each fight off the frenzy of careening ice cubes to down their drinks in one go, and head home to recover. Little do George and Gracie realize that in their haste to leave, they mistook a decorative door painted on a wall of the bar for the real thing. The patrons of the H-Bar, though, are well accustomed to people passing through walls and hardly take note of George and Gracie's abrupt departure.

"A century ago, while Conrad and Freud were illuminating the heart and the soul of darkness, Max Planck shed the first ray of light on quantum mechanics, a conceptual framework that proclaims, among other things, that the H-Bar experiences of George and Gracie- when scaled down to the microscopic realm- need not be attributed to clouded faculties. Such unfamiliar and bizarre happenings are typical of how our universe, on extremely small scales, actually behaves."

Well this tunneling that occurs is real and happens on a microscopic scale. It happens everyday, all the time; it is part of the process in our brains and is intimate to the fabric of reality. Intimate to our conscious perceptions and to how we affect things and people around us.

Another oddity of quantum mechanics is that taking measurements affects the outcome. That is, the very act of measuring something will affect what the outcome will be. This has been proven. I now go to Evan Harris's book once more, this time on page 136. Bold markings of the letters are my doing.

"We got into the measurement problem in the first place because quantum mechanics seems to be saying that **observers really affect the things that they observed**--because quantum mechanics tells us that **physical properties have, in general, no objective reality independent of the act of observation.** As Pascual Jordan, one of the major contributors to quantum theory, put it, 'Observations not only disturb what has to be measured, they produce it...We compel (the electron) to assume a definite position...We ourselves produce the results of measurement.'

Maybe the way out is to accept the fact that hidden variables, in any usual sense of the term, are not going to solve the problem. Maybe we need simply accept the fact that the observer (the consciousness, for observer is just a euphemism for this concept) actually exists as a participatory constituent of physical reality."

Yes what is consciousness? That feeling that you can step back from yourself and observe yourself. That feeling that you are inhabiting a body like wearing a suit. The spark of recognition behind the reality of the physical form. The perception of that painting on the wall being something other than what it actually was. The perception of a smell where there is nothing to smell, the perception of seeing things you shouldn't be able to see, feeling another persons emotions, or personality, and even at times, their thoughts. Feeling the energy exchange between you and another as your frequencies mesh and interact.

I saw a bumper sticker once that seemed as if it had consciousness all figured out. It may have as well, at least for many people, it said, "Consciousness - that annoying time between naps." Well let's see where Dr. Harris takes us now on this journey. On page151 he begins to describe consciousness:

"Consciousness is not thinking. Consciousness is not thinking about one's consciousness. It is not self-reflection. Consciousness needs no words and needs no things. Those born blind or deaf and mute, they are as conscious as you and I. A fly blankly staring at a red table cloth in a red room will have redness consciousness...Consciousness is not perception, or wakefulness, or attention, even though these are all so closely linked that a week's arguing and discussing may not be enough to tease apart and illuminate these related ideas...Of course, we are ordinarily conscious when awake and, except for dreaming, are ordinarily not conscious when asleep..."

"...Consciousness is the blue of the sky; it is C sharp, the taste of sweetness as it fills the mind, the smell of gardenia, the pain of love that is lost, the experienced murmuring brook as it is, the moon reflected in the pool...But consciousness is not thinking. Consciousness is the carrier of conscious thought. It is what's left when thought is removed, when mind is stilled. When thought is entirely gone, the consciousness is still there in the void......as the channel capacity of consciousness."

On page 181 Dr. Walker goes on:

"We have the word consciousness, but it is difficult to communicate just what even this means to another person unless that person has experienced on his own the same questions about his inner nature. And if that person has not, you might as well try to communicate with a tree stump."

On page 182 he continues:

"Consciousness is not so many atoms. It does not consist of photons or quarks. Neither is it molecules spinning about in the brain. Consciousness is something that exists in its own right.

"And yet consciousness does interact in some way, by some connection, with the things of the physical world that physicists measure, know and describe."..."What is the fundamental physical quantity that links consciousness, a thing in its own right, to material phenomena?"

On page 186, "What we need are the tools that will enable us to look at this world with a razor eye of a Newton or an Einstein so that we can discover the pieces that form that theory. I emphasize the word theory because it is so much misunderstood, so often misused to refer to almost any nascent idea as though it were synonymous with hypothesis, conjecture, or notion. Theory, as the word is intended to be used in science, refers to a conception of the nature of some set of phenomena that fits all the facts and that has survived the tests of time and experiment. Experiments give us raw data. Theory, and only theory, gives us understanding."

Dr. Walker goes on to enumerate a shopping list of things to check that might link the mind and the brain to connect consciousness to the physical world. In so doing, he eliminates force fields, gravitation, strong and weak nuclear forces, and electromagnetic forces and arrives at a Quantum mechanical connection. In order to find that link, he looks into the machinery of the brain and he finds, in the synapse, a place to look (remember that Dr. Walker has also made major contributions in neurophysiology as well as physics, psychology and medicine). On page 194 we read Dr. Walker once more:

"To find the quantum mechanical link, we will have to look elsewhere. We will have to look in the machinery of the key component of the brain computer; we will have to look into its basic switching element, the synapse. There we will find how quantum mechanical tunneling plays a subtle but essential role in the triggering of these switches. There, in those minute switches, at the minuscule intersynaptic cleft-that is where the quantitative link between mind and brain is to be found. That is where the first test came and where the fit between an incipient idea stirring in my mind first met the physical evidence that, as we will see, makes this concept so immediately apparent. It came so smoothly together that I knew this must be the secret doorway into the mind."

Remember Gracie and George in the story from Brian Greene's book? Remember the cigar through the back of the head and the ice cubes through the glass? This is the quantum tunneling that Dr. Walker speaks of happening. This type of activity in the brain in the synapses. He takes us through the logic, and the science, of how this must be, and how it has to be. He takes us through the way we calculate the minimum firing rate of synapses to have consciousness, and the shortest interval of consciousness, and our data capacity. Our data capacity alone is an amazing thing at 50 million bits per second. He does all this since he says on page 199, "But if we are going to find out just what consciousness is and how it works, we must be able to show that our quantum mechanical ideas lead to some meaningful, testable, predictable, falsifiable results. We are going to need numbers. We will somehow "measure" consciousness."

Dr. Walker takes us through a lesson in basic neurology to run the numbers to see what is, and isn't, possible in the interactions of synapses with quantum tunneling. The result being that quantum tunneling is in fact possible, and necessary, for consciousness to occur. The results of testing are checked against the theory and the result is a perfect fit. The theory explaining the data obtained from the experiments.

On page 237 he concludes what consciousness is:

"Consciousness is not this set of objects or electrons, as such, at all. These exist to bring into being the potential interactions- the quantum potentialities-that are the state vectors. Consciousness is the collection of potentialities that develop as these electrons and these structures of the brain interact. Consciousness is the bringing about of this ongoing state vector of possibilities that runs through the brain...By creating the possibilities that we experience as consciousness and by selecting-by willing- which synapse will fire, mind brings into reality each moments thoughts, experiences and actions."

Then on page 256:

"Consciousness may also exist somewhere without being a part of either a living body or a data-processing system. Indeed, because everything that exists is ultimately the result of one or more quantum mechanical events, the universe is inhabited by an almost unlimited number of rather discrete, conscious, usually nonthinking entities. These conscious entities determine singly the outcome of each quantum mechanical event, whereas the Schrodinger equation constrains their freedom of action collectively.

For the first time in our history of wondering who and what we are, we have a way to find the answers. We have a way to know the truth, and we have taken a step toward the realization of that hope. We can see this quantum mind of each of us is part of the fabric of reality.

But there is another part of the mind, something beyond consciousness, something incredible, and something that is already within our grasp. It is something that shows why our minds transcend being machines. It is the true wellspring of our identity. It is our link to the infinite."

And this is why I have led you on this lengthy journey of Walker's. This concept and his scientific investigation now lead us to the tie that we have to creation. This tie is the way that we create our own reality daily. The way our perceptions are influenced and our experiences created. Indulge me a bit further by exercising your will to proceed as the conclusion of this story of Dr. Walker is probably one of the most profound conclusions one can arrive at. It is the glue that puts all the mysteries together. It ties the Mystics and the Shaman and the ancient beliefs of religions around the world into the reality of our present day living here in the 21st century. A bit more patience and I think you will be pleased at the result. On page 263 Dr. Walker speaks of the will:

"You will remember in Chapter 12 we talked about a quantity we simply called Q. It's a number. It tells us how many other synapses one synapse can influence quantum mechanically. One synapse has the ability to cause to fire any one of the many possible synapses associated by means of the quantum mechanical interaction. You will remember that we calculated the value of Q and we found it to be 200,000. Now the chance that any one of these synapses will fire is 1/200,000.(that is 1/Q) . Using this probability of 1/Q we can easily calculate just how much information is "input" every time one synapse fires by means of this quantum mechanical interaction. The result is 17.6 bits of information. Now this happens at a rate of once every 0.3 milliseconds. Therefore, we can get the information rate by dividing by this time. The result is just under 60,000 bits per second. That is the channel capacity of the will. **This will is what we really are. Let me say that again. This will is what we really are**. We will soon find this will information capacity to be an extremely important quantity, so let us call this number W, just as we have called the conscious channel capacity C. C is what we experience; W is what we are.

"There is another quantity that we will find to be quite important. It is the amount of will information in one "frame of the film", so to speak, through which we see ultimate reality. We showed in the last chapter that there is a characteristic interval of time over which our consciousness is smeared, a time of about 0.04 second. This is the length of the tick of the consciousness clock. You will remember that in Chapters 11 and 13, in addition to the consciousness data rate, we obtained a quantity F, which we called the information content of the consciousness at any moment. The consciousness channel capacity, C, consists of frames or images with data content, F. Correspondingly, for the will data rate, W we calculate a will filed, which we denote by the letter G. We get the value of G by multiplying the will data rate by the consciousness time tick of 0.04 second. This gives a value for G of nearly 25400 bits. Make a note of these four measures of the mind.....Let's Summarize the values of these quantities because we will be referring back to them:

Consciousness stream	C	47.5 million bits/second
Will Stream	W	58.7 thousand bits/second
Conscious moment	F	1.90 million bits
Will moment	G	2.35 thousand bits

"...The will is the channel that determines what our next move, choice, and thought will be. It selects the path our mind takes through the images of the things the brain scatters before us. The will is our innermost nature; our being that is there when the things we might see go blank. It may even be there when all else is gone...but for that, we must await more understanding. **It is perhaps this aspect of the mind that comes to the fore when one is in deep meditation, a state of consciousness designed to remove thoughts and sensory contact with the world.**

But there is something more. From what we have already seen in the past chapters, from what we know to be the nature of state selection on observation in the quantum mechanical process of state vector collapse, and from the surprising characteristics proven in the tests of Bell's theorem, we should immediately see just what W means and what we have in the will data channel.

Before an event occurs in quantum mechanics, objects have interacted and entered into a set of potentialities, the states of quantum mechanics. After observation, on state vector collapse, everything goes into one state. Everything. No matter where the objects are. This is the incredible discovery that the tests of Bell's theorem prove. When a particular synapse, among the 200,000 possible synapses fires, everything else- everywhere in the whole universe- that might be tied to that choice by the will channel must also go into that same overall quantum mechanical state! Unlike the consciousness, our will is not restricted to the tiny space of the brain cavity. Everything we touch, see, experience in any way becomes caught up in that special aspect of the quantum nature of matter and will retain a link back to our mind. And observation of it or our subsequent observation of its consequences can impact on the state that it is in. **The will channel is a link that transcends space, and because physicists have found that something called Lorentz invariance always holds, this will must transcend time as well."**

Wow is about all I can say to that but he continues to awe me confounding the thought of it on page 265.

"What we are saying is this will channel causes the events in the brain and those in the external world to go hand in hand with what happens in our consciousness. We are saying that our mind can affect matter-even other brains-and that distant matter and minds can have an effect on us. What we have here, what is forced on us by the formalism of quantum mechanics itself, is something that sounds like telepathy or psycho kinesis; it is exactly what Einstein feared to be the implications of Quantum mechanics. Why is it so elusive? Why does it seem so strange? Because the signal, W, is so small compared to the noise of our everyday consciousness given by C. That is, because the signal to noise ratios, W/C, is very small. What we have found in our quest for the tangible fabric of reality has carried us past objectivity, beyond mind even, and into the realm of things paranormal!"

"In all of this, the observer is tied to all observers, and these observers collectively select the reality that occurs. But much more, the observer-the perfect observer-always gets what he or she wants. Indeed, for the perfect observer, there cannot exist even the concept of desiring a state (from among those that quantum mechanics permits to occur) without that state at the same instant becoming reality. We do not explain how these state selections happen-at least not for a few more pages. Rather, this is the nature of observation. What we can point out, however is that we are not perfect observers. Our desires that are a part of our consciousness are not always a part of the will channel that could bring them into being. We do not always have, as the mystics might put it, a perfect purity of mind and heart.

"Instead our ability to distinguish the will channel, from all the thoughts of our consciousness, as a means to affect outside occurrences is nearly nil. This is the discovery locked up in the numbers for W, the will channel, and C, our consciousness channel. Both of these channels are part of the mind. Both stem from the same kind of things, quantum mechanical events going on at the synapses. Our will images are so dim compared to those of our daily conscious existence that they are almost always lost in the torrent of our consciousness stream. You see the quantity W measures the channel capacity that can affect things and events, directly and globally, through space and through time. But the quantity C, our consciousness stream of information about the world here and now, is, as far as such efforts are concerned just so much noise. We may experience our desire to influence an object or contact the mind of another. It may enter our consciousness, C, but it will have no effect there. Thus, W is the measure of the signal that can do these things; C is the measure of the noise to which we misdirect our efforts; and

A New Reality

W/C is the signal to noise ratio. Its value is small: 0.00124 using the values of W and C we gave earlier. It says that if one tries over and over to determine the flip of a coin ahead of time, one probably will succeed by means of this perfect channel only once in a thousand tries. All else will, be the result of chance. But that one try is not a try. The wish is the completed fact. The word is a perfect act."

So what does this mean? We need to turn off the chatter to gain control of the influence of the will. Then, what we will, will be. Literally.

Does this explain how miracles occur? Possibly. You decide. Does it explain ESP, mysticism, telekinesis, or offer the possibility that such things can happen? Does it explain our dog knowing when my wife is coming home, or Beth knowing when I'm in need of help ,or my dad knowing when something's wrong with one of his sons? Does it explain the perceptions we have not always being what's perceived by others? Possibly, you decide. It very well might.

At least for one, I feel more and more comfortable that the things that have occurred in my life, have not been some delusion, or result of a nervous breakdown or something. I now feel that the world is something quite different from what I had previously perceived it to be through the blinders of our "accepted" and non questioning life style. Again I seemed to have come across the information I needed to help me clear up some questions and reinforce my new beliefs and viewpoint of life. I hope it has done the same for you, and if not, at least opened the door to further possibilities for you. Maybe it even upset you to be such a deviation from your beliefs. If you felt anger then that too is good, as anger can show you where you have a problem to resolve (though I really don't mean to get you upset. That really is your decision, not mine).

I used to think it strange that such people as Shirley Maclaine (fabulous actress and author of the controversial book and movie "Out on a Limb" and several other intriguing books) would be friends with one of the foremost authorities in the field of physics. That is, Stephen Hawkings. Likewise the famous Psychiatrist Dr. Carl Jung would have dinner with a friend of his named Albert Einstein. Now I know why such seemingly unrelated professions can have such an attraction to each other. There is quite a connection between them.

The artistry of Shirley Maclaine and the soft side of science in psychiatry mixing with the intensely numerical and rigorously methodical world of physics. Now I can see why and I also can see why no one ever hears about what is discussed there. How could most physicists ever face their peers when discussing such matters as Evan Harris Walker has so bravely and eloquently discussed and put the magnifying glass and razor edge of an Einstein, as he says, to this matter. Thank you Dr. Walker.

Book Listing

Instead of just including a standard bibliography I felt it would be more helpful to include a booklist with descriptions of the books as well.

(In no particular Order.)

Rings of Truth - A true story, about the author, that was fictionalized by the author for readability. A man that came from being poor and unhappy to being rich and unhappy to being whole and happy and loved. A wonderful tale that touches the heart and soul.

The Road Less Traveled - A book by a Doctor of Psychiatry about confronting and solving problems, discipline, love, growth and religion and grace.

The Road Less Traveled and Beyond - The latest book from the author of the book above. It is about spiritual growth in an age of anxiety. This man puts it all together nicely in this book. He establishes the need for thinking again. In a society that has given over their decisions to everyone else by following established roads Dr. Peck re-ignites the need for genius and thinking about life daily. How the lack of thought causes the inequity and injustice's and prejudices in life.

The Tenth Insight, Holding the Vision an Experiential Guide - An exciting, revealing, motivating book that wasn't meant as a motivating book. An aid in exploring oneself. A book about the changes some people are experiencing in this day and age. The increased consciousness and the chance happenings and meeting of people. An extension of Carl Jung's Synchronisity theory.

The Celestine Prophecy an Experiential Guide - A guide book to learn more about yourself and the world around you. A companion to the best selling novel, The Celestine Prophecy. Again, a book about the changes some people are experiencing in this day and age. The increased consciousness and the chance happenings and meeting of people. An extension of Carl Jung's Synchronisity theory.

The Celestine Vision - The historic and scientific background of our current planetary awakening and how we can grow in it.

Emmanuel's Book II - The Choice For Love - A look at love and fear as opposites and how you can choose between which of the two you want in your life. Excellent food for thought.

Practical Intuition For Success. - A new way to approach business or personal decisions using your sixth sense.

The Elegant Universe - A book about physics that is written to be readable by non physicists. Ties together what Einstein tried to do till the day he died but never did. It ties together the mysteries of Einstein's General Relativity and Quantum Mechanics. It explains the growth of both and the implications of them. Multiple dimensions are given to the reader as fodder for thought on what it could mean. Yes there are dimensions beyond the 4 (height, length, width, and time) that we perceive.

A Journey Through the Tenth Dimension - An audio tape of a physicist giving a presentation on Quantum Mechanics and General Relativity. Comedic and mind expanding. This may be in book form as well. Similar to The Elegant Universe **in** nature.

The Physics Of Consciousness - A book on Quantum Physics as it relates to consciousness and our perceptions. Written by Evan Harris Walker who is the founder and director of the Walker Cancer Institute has made major scientific contributions in astronomy, physics, neurophysiology, psychology and medicine. Holds a PHD in physics and has published more than a hundred papers in scientific journals and magazines and holds a dozen patents.

The Seat of the Soul - A national bestseller that is a wonderful book written by a scientist (Quantum physicist) with a philosophers heart. It's about achieving true authentic power. Gary has been a frequent visitor to Oprah Winfrey's show and has written mind opening books.

The Re-Enchantment of Everyday Life. - Thomas Moore, was a monk in a Catholic religious order and has degrees in theology, musicology and philosophy and has written several other books of much value as well. The book is about how to restore the heart and soul of everyday living.

Care of The Soul - written by the same author as the book listed just above this one. It is a guide for cultivating depth and sacredness in everyday life.

Book Of Shadows - Written by a woman lawyer about her awakening that there was more to life than was apparent and how she put this power to use for her to help others and herself.

Transforming the Mind - Written by one of the great spiritual leaders of all time, the Dalai Lama himself about how to generate compassion. Written by one with a great respect of diversity and a belief in the need for a questioning mindset.

Traveling With Power - A well written true story about the development and exploration of perception from a Vietnam vet that becomes trained as a Shaman

Joshua, A Parable for Today - A national bestseller written by a priest that has a result that many priests wouldn't have had the courage to write.

A Course in Miracles, Text, Workbook for Students, Manual for Teachers - Everything you ever wanted to know about miracles. Very detailed and somewhat hard to read but with valuable insight. Be ready to think clearly.

Conversations With God - A journalist has conversations with God who explains everything to us is a series of books by the same name. Whether you believe it is God speaking to him, or not, it is interesting food for thought. Numerous books by this author and all very good and entertaining as well as mind opening.

The Witches Way- Principles, Rituals and Beliefs of Modern Witchcraft - A well written book that takes some of the fear and mystery out of what witchcraft is and who are its tenants. I found it best to start the book on page 105 however to get an overview before going into the rituals at the beginning.

Your Sixth Sense - Activating Your Psychic Potential - Belleruth Naparstek, a practicing Psychotherapist for over 30 years and a mother of 3 investigates 45 different people (12 PhD's, 4 MD.'s and 9 MA.'s, that are psychotherapists, physicians, nurses, corporate trainers, medical intuitives, engineers and on and on) She surveys them and profiles what their characteristics are that make them intuitive and relates this to how someone might develop this talent in them selves. Right brain and left brain attributes and so on.

On the next page, are the details of the books should you want to take this to the bookstore or look them up online. Again these are only a few books. Some were referenced in the book and others were not. There will be many others that may attract you in the same area as you will find these. Tear the next two pages out and put it in your wallet if you like.

Books are just books but if you don't use them they are nothing. Go ahead. Tear the page out (as long as it's not someone else's book that is).

Bibliography

Jim Britt with Eve Hogan, **Rings Of Truth** . (Grass Valley California: Master Key Productions Inc., 1998)

M.Scott Peck, M.D., **The Road Less Traveled.** (New York: A touchstone book by Simon and Schuster, 1978)

M.Scott Peck, M.D., **The Road Less Traveled and Beyond.** (New York: Touchstone, 1997)

James Redfield and Carol Adrienne, **The Tenth Insight, Holding the Vision, An Experiential Guide.** (Ney York: Warner Books, 1996)

James Redfiled and Carol Adrienne, **The Celestine Prophecy, An Experiential Guide** (New York: Warner Books, 1994)

James Redfield, **The Celestine Vision.** (New York: Warner Books, 1997)

Pat Rodegast and Judith Stanton, **Emmanuel's Book II The Choice For Love.** (New York: Bantam and Bantam Audio publishing, 1989) (In book and audio tape)

Laura Day, **Practical Intuition For Success.** (New York: Harper Audio and Harper Collins, 1997) (In book and audio tape)

Brian Greene, **The Elegant Universe.** (New York, London: W.W. Norton & Company 1999.)

Michio Kaku, **A Journey Through the Tenth Dimension.** (New York: Mystic Fire Audio, 1990)

A New Reality

Evan Harris Walker, **The Physics of Consciousness**
(Cambridge, Mass: Perseus Books, 1999)

Gary Zukav, **The Seat of the Soul.** (New York: Simon and
Schuster 1989)

Thomas Moore, **The Re-Enchantment of Everyday Life.**
(New York: Harper Collins, 1996)

Thomas Moore, **Care of The Soul.** (New York: Harper
Collins 1994)

Phyllis Curott, **Book of Shadows.** (New York: Broadway
Books, 1998)

His Holiness The Dalai Lama, **Transforming the Mind,**
Teachings in Generating Compassion. (London:
Thornsons 2000 an imprint of Harper Collins, 2000)

Ken Eagle Feather, **Traveling With Power.** (Charlottesville,
VA., Hampton Roads Publishing Company, Inc., 1996)

Joseph F. Girzone, **Joshua.** (New York: Simon & Schuster,
1987)

The foundation for Inner Peace, **A Course in Miracles,**
Text, Workbook for Students, Manual for Teachers.
(New York: Penguin Books, 1996)

Neale Donald Walsch, **Conversations With God.** (New
York: Putnam Publishing Group, 1996)

Janet and Stewart Farrar, **The Witches Way- Principles,**
Rituals and Beliefs of Modern Witchcraft (Custer,
Washington: Phoenix Publishing Inc., 1984)

A.J. Aaron

Belleruth Naparstek, **Your Sixth Sense - Activating Your Psychic Potential** (New York: HarperCollins Publishers Inc.1997).